Confessions of a Space Cadet:

The Transformation of a Teacher

HAMILTON PRESS

LANHAM • NEW YORK • LONDON

Copyright © 1987 by

Hamilton Press

4720 Boston Way
Lanham, MD 20706

3 Henrietta Street
London WC2E 8LU England

British Cataloging in Publication Information Available

Library of Congress Cataloging-in-Publication Data

Carter, John Marshall.
    Confessions of a space cadet.

    1. Carter, John Marshall.   2. Teachers—United
States—Biography.   I. Title.
LA2317.C34A3   1987   371.1'0092'4 [B]   87-8472
ISBN 0-8191-6329-5 (alk. paper)
ISBN 0-8191-6330-9 (pbk. : alk. paper)

All Hamilton Press books are produced on acid-free
paper which exceeds the minimum standards set by the National
Historical Publication and Records Commission.

Hamilton Press

This book is dedicated to my wife, Suzon

TABLE OF CONTENTS

INTRODUCTION: WHAT MAKES A GOOD TEACHER?

In 1983, A NATION AT RISK floored almost everyone. American Education was exposed and certain revelations gave even the most ardent defender reason to shudder. Numerous plans of action have since been prescribed in the past four years and surely more will come as the nation prepares to cure the ills of education.

Nineteen eighty-five was proclaimed "The Year of the Teacher." The president of the United States, in an effort to bring public attention to the teaching profession and the dedicated professionals who populate its ranks, suggested that a teacher in space might give the profession the desired public visibility. Sharon Christa McAuliffe, a New Hampshire social studies teacher, was chosen from hundreds of aspirants by the National Aeronautics and Space Administration to fly on the space shuttle as a representative of teachers everywhere. The tragic events of January 28, 1986 do not erase the heroic sacrifice of Christa McAuliffe. They only underscore the point that within the ranks of A NATION AT RISK are dedicated men and women who give so much of themselves to their students and their communities.

What is a space cadet? Since the book displays that title, the question is appropriate. It is hoped that the answer will be presented in the book. For starters, though, I will say the way that I am using Space Cadet is not in a pejorative sense. To me, a teacher Space Cadet (and I would like to think that the finalists in the "Teacher in Space" competition had such qualities) is a teacher who is so dedicated to the profession, to teaching students, to searching out new ways of solving problems, that he/she is quite often mistaken for the other type of Space Cadet. This confusion occurs because certain teachers (the real Space Cadets) appear to be on different wavelengths from the great majority of their colleagues in the profession.

In this book I hope to give yet another answer to the question "What Makes a Good Teacher?" With merit pay plans, assessment, and curriculum development on everyone's lips these days, I would like to offer my story of one type of teacher who, I believe, is a true professional and who may be able to take some of the risks out

1

of A NATION AT RISK.

In my development as a teacher, I have had the help and expertise of many fine individuals. I would like to name them all, but the need for brevity forbids it. However, I will name some of them here. First of all, thanks to all the Space Cadets who taught me. I owe you more than I can ever repay. To my parents, Mr. and Mrs. Howard C. Carter, thanks and love. A special note of thanks to my brother, Richard Carter, who really got me on the road to teaching. To my sister, Annette, and her husband Charles Strader, thanks for all of the meals at the S&W Cafeteria that sustained me during my undergraduate days at Elon College.

A thank-you to some special teachers along the way: Louise Shumate and Dr. Blanche Norman of Burton Grove Elementary School; Lucy Reynolds Beecher of Leaksville-Spray Junior High School; Wendell Owen, principal of Leaksville-Spray Junior High School; Julia Ivie, Sarah Rodgers and Dr. Bruce Barnes of Morehead High School in Leaksville (now Eden), North Carolina; J.C. Honeycutt and Dr. Alton Thompson of the Eden City Schools; Dr. James P. Elder, Jr., Dr. Robert W. Delp, and Coach Bill Miller of Elon College; Dr. George Hall, Bill Bradshaw, and others in Windsor, Virginia; Dr. Bennett D. Hill, O.S.B., St. Anselm's Abbey, Washington, D.C.; Mr. Joe Old, Chicago, Illinois; Dr. Stephen Fritz of East Tennessee State University; the late Professor Emeritus John Beeler, Dr. Russell Planck, Dr. Karl Schleunes and Dr. Richard Bardolph of the University of North Carolina at Greensboro; Dr. R. Baird Shuman, University of Illinois at Urbana-Champaign; Dr. R.F. Saunders, Jr., Dr. Charles S. Thomas, Dr. Vernon Egger, Dr. Jay Fraser, Professor Richard Tichich, and Dr. Harry Carter of Georgia Southern College in Statesboro, Georgia; Nancy Osborne, Geraldine Fincannon, Dr. Joseph Milner, Dr. Jim Dervin, and other members of the 1982 Wake Forest University Writing Project; Rachel Wright, Ed Egan and the Wampus Cats of Eden, North Carolina; Dr. Angelo Volpe, Vice Chancellor for Academic Affairs, East Carolina University; Dr. Hugh Wease, and other colleagues of mine in the history department at East Carolina University; Dr. Charles Coble, Dr. Patricia Terrell, and Dr. Patricia Anderson of the School of Education, East

Carolina Universisty; Mr. Henry Macintosh and Mr. Peter Burke, Southern Regional Examinations Board, Southhampton, United Kingdom; Dr. Arnd Krüger and the staff of the Institut für Sportwissenschaften at the University of Göttingen, West Germany. A thank-you also to Mr. and Mrs. Richard Robertson of THE EDEN DAILY NEWS for their willingness to publish educational material about teaching, teachers, and students. There are so many others: thanks to my old fantasy writing partner, Danny Squires. Thank-yous are also in order to Ellen Turlington Johnston-Hale, Dr. Denny Wolfe, and Dr. Robert Reising. I would be remiss if I did not say thanks to the Druid Dudes of East Carolina University with whom I write, talk about writing, and run the give and go at lunch-time.

I would surely be remiss if I did not remember my friends and colleagues in the Cumberland County Schools, a place that I have thought fondly of since leaving there in 1978. To Wendle Capps and the Capps' Cowboys (and Cowgirls) at Westover Junior High School, to Dr. Bill Shipp of Westover Senior High School, and to administrators H. James Hankins, who helped me tremendously, Jack Freeman, Benny Pearce, and all other veterans of Middle School Conferences everywhere, thanks to you all. I would also like to mention individuals in the North Carolina State Department of Education who have helped and inspired me along the way: Jean Blackmon, the late C.C. Lipscomb, and Raymond Rhodes.

Thanks go to Professor R. Baird Shuman of the University of Illinois for reading the entire manuscript and making numerous suggestions that saved me from many errors. However, whatever errors that remain in this book are mine alone.

Special thanks to Mrs. Agnes Jones for typing a draft of the manuscript and to Mrs. Becky Latham for typing the final draft.

I would like to acknowledge the invaluable support of Cheryl Keesee of the Hamilton Press.

A special thank you to my parents-in-law, Mr. and Mrs. Robert B. Grogan of Eden, North Carolina, their daughter Sherry B. Grogan and her husband Abdullah Kahlil Abu-Hashem. I must not forget my

3

daughter, Alyson. And, to my wife, Suzon, the greatest supporter of them all, thanks!

CHAPTER ONE
THE DAN RIVER GRADUATE
"BASEBALL IS A GAME OF GOING HOME."

Saucy Catlett had never liked his given name. He once confessed to me that he could not see why his parents had given him the names they did. I can hear him now: "Of all the names they had to call me Howard Cecil Catlett." "Saucy" quickly shed the appellations Howard Cecil. Only his father, old Winfred Catlett, continued to call him Howard. First his name was H.C. and, finally, after establishing his reputation as a debonair Ladies-Man-in-Chief, the tag Saucy stuck.

Aside from disliking his name, the only other thing Saucy disliked was his $5 a week paycheck — a typical wage for a mundane task in a southern cotton mill during the 1930s. Saucy lived in Leaksville, North Carolina, a small mill town in the northwestern piedmont area of the state. Leaksville grew up beside the Dan River, a moderate-sized stream which had its source in the foothills of southwestern Virginia. Saucy's life revolved around the Dan: the mill where he worked overlooked the river, evenings after work he fished in the river, and he spent many lifetimes wishing he could see the river empty into the ocean.

Raising two kids on five dollars a week was no easy task, but life was easier to swallow in the South in the 1930s than it would have been elsewhere. Or, at least that's the way the mosaic Saucy paints for me looks everytime we're on our way trout fishing. Being a post-war baby, I sometimes yearn for Saucy's simpler 1930s.

Those times provided Saucy with a full, rich life--going to church on Sundays, drinking with the boys after work, playing basketball and baseball at the Y.M.C.A., and tending to the chores of domestic bliss. But, five dollars a week was not exactly the economic security Saucy had in mind. The only alternative for a sixth grade graduate, of what Saucy called Burton Grove Seminary, was to join the industrial pilgrimage to Wilmington--to work in the naval shipyard. Hundreds from Leaksville, Spray and Draper had left family and friends behind to give shipbuilding a whirl. Shucks, Briar Wilkes and the Reynolds boys had gone. Puddin' Fuller, Stacy Soots, De Kook, and their wives and children had trekked to the promising Promised Land. "Why not?" thought the quixotic Saucy.

As Saucy and family rolled across the Cape Fear River into Wilmington, Saucy looked northward and was amazed at the long row of ships he saw there. "Look Mama," he effused boyishly! "There must be a whole war fleet here," Saucy screamed, not knowing that the river was decked out in a merchant marine garb. There wasn't a gunboat or an aircraft carrier in sight.

Wilmington staggered Saucy's and Mama's imagination. To them it was a metropolis. Leaksville had had only 2,500 people.

Saucy, Mama, and the kids found a battered Dickensesque flat for fifty cents a week. Saucy unloaded the A Model and proceeded confidently to the shipyard.

After an hour of following difficult directions, Saucy finally dragged his hot and sweaty frame into the office of the Director of Personnel. He saw a sign which glared:

APPLICATIONS ACCEPTED

His heart pounded. A pretty, schoolgirlish secretary directed him to the director's office, and the office of a Mr. Hiram Skowers.

Skowers talked on and on about many subjects Saucy didn't understand. He never looked at Saucy. Saucy didn't like that. His daddy, old Winfred, had taught him always to look at the one to whom you're talking. Saucy deduced that Skowers must be a Yankee (even though his accent was hard to decipher) or had no upbringing or both. Yankees were thought to be heathens and debauched revellers.

Skowers finally decided to get to the point. "Mr. Catlett, you said you're interested in becoming a pipe-fitter," he asked. "Yes sirree," said Saucy, trying to smother Skowers with Southern Gentility but feeling that Skowers was not susceptible to it. "I worked in the boiler room in a mill in Leaksville for years," added Saucy confidently as he grinned like a mule that finally got the carrot. "I can fit pipes as easy as Grant took Richmond," Saucy prodded! "You may recall, Mr. Catlett, that General Grant experienced quite a great deal of

6

difficulty with his invasion of the South," Skowers remarked trying to demonstrate his intellectual superiority. "What is your educational background, Mr. Catlett?" inquired Skowers. "You are a high school graduate, aren't you Mr. Catlett?" he probed.

"It's like this, Mr. Skowers . . .," Saucy said as he dropped his chin. Before he could finish the sentence, the childlike secretary interrupted. "I'm sorry Mr. Skowers, but the Under Secretary of the Navy is on the phone!" she said.

"Quite all right, Miss Vernon," Skowers stammered. "I'll take it in my office," he added. "And the telephone call, too?" kidded Miss Vernon as a broad, mischievous grin covered her face. Skowers blushed, looked perturbed and told Saucy to come back in two days. Saucy almost giggled at Miss Vernon's insinuation but stifled it.

Saucy assured me that miracles happened then. Maybe they still do. Saucy said that as he was sitting in the Riverside Cafe, he heard someone yell a familiar yell: "Saucy, you old son-of-a-gun," was the cry. Saucy grinned widely as he saw an old face. Seeing a familiar face can warm a soul in a foreign land. It was his old Y.M.C.A. basketball buddy, Arthur Weiskopf the Good Yankee--the transplant, as Saucy like to call him. "Whitehead (those were the only German words Saucy knew), what are you doing in Wilmington?" Saucy beamed. "I was transferred here by my insurance firm--I'm a manager," Weiskopf admitted modestly. Saucy said that Arthur was quiet and reserved. "What are you doing here, Saucy?" Arthur asked with some unusual enthusiasm. "To tell you the truth, old buddy, my family and I are looking for a new start," said Saucy. "Leaksville was beginning to smother me; everything was all right, but everything was all wrong," Saucy tried to explain. "I need a job badly," he added.

"What field are you trying?" questioned Arthur. "Shipbuilding," Saucy snapped quickly. "I'm here to get in on some of that government money," Saucy said like an experienced conniver, which he wasn't.

"Do you know anyone down at personnel at the shipyard Whitey," Saucy asked? "As a matter of fact, I went to college with a fellow there named Hiram Skowers--we used to call him Hi-Skow," Arthur exclaimed. Saucy couldn't believe it. "You're kidding!" Saucy blurted excitedly. "I have an appointment with him on Friday, about a job as a pipefitter!" Saucy said. "That should be a snap for you," Arthur said encouragingly.

"Tell you what Saucy, I'll call Hiram tonight and tell him to give my old pal a good look!" Arthur said. "If you're qualified, he'll give you a job," Arthur added. "Where'd you go to college, Sauce?" Arthur asked. Arthur never knew that Saucy was one of seventeen children. The Y.M.C.A. had a way of equalizing everyone. Arthur moved away from Leaksville years ago. He had no idea that Saucy was a sixth grade graduate of Burton Grove Seminary. "Huh, Saucy, where'd you go?" Arthur asked again.

Saucy thought quickly. "C.C. and W.M.," he said quickly, trying to look unmoved by Arthur's questioning. "Great!" said Arthur. "No problem," Arthur bellowed in an unusual show of emotion. "Hi-Skow won't be able to turn down a man who has both a high school diploma and a degree from C.C. and W.M."

Saucy worried for two days. He had, of course, failed to mention to his friend Arthur that C.C. and W.M. stood for Carolina Cotton and Woolen Mill. But, he finally decided that it was useless to worry anymore. If he got the job, fine; if he didn't, he didn't.

It all seemed too easy that Friday morning. Miss Vernon was particularly accommodating and charming as she directed Saucy to Skowers' office. "Good morning, Mr. Catlett," beamed Skowers. "I understand you attended Carolina College and finished at William and Mary," he related his homework. "Are you sure a pipefitter's job is what you want?" Skowers continued without giving Saucy a chance to answer the initial question. "Yes, that will be fine," Saucy mumbled as he tried to keep from looking at Skowers squarely.

"You got it boy!" Skowers exclaimed extending his hand to Saucy. "Go by room 204 and get your uniforms and tool box," he instructed.

"Thank you, sir," Saucy said as he shuffled toward the door. "Six-thirty--tomorrow!" Skowers commanded in a kidding manner.

"Right!" replied Saucy.

Saucy phoned Weiskopf's office that afternoon when he got home. "Arthur, I just wanted to call and say thanks," Saucy mumbled humbly. "Don't mention it," reassured Arthur. "Just keep ole Hi-Skow happy," Arthur added. "Well, got to run, Sauce, client's on the other phone," Arthur said hurriedly! "One more thing, Sauce," Arthur quipped. "I've heard of U.C.L.A., U.N.C., N.Y.U. and other abbreviations for colleges and universities, but what and where is C.C. and W.M.?" Arthur inquired. "Carolina Cotton and Woolen Mills - bye Arthur!" Saucy yelled and slammed down the phone. "Saucy!" Saaauuuccccyyyyyyyy!" Arthur screamed at the whirring of no one . . .

Arthur never told Skowers about Saucy. Saucy worked at the shipyard as a pipefitter for two years. He then was promoted to foreman of a whole crew of pipefitters. He held that position for another year and a half.

One day Saucy could not bear to board another tin can. He, Mama, and the two kids packed the A Model and headed for Leaksville. Saucy returned to his old "alma mater," C.C. and W.M., and stayed there faithfully for three more years.

Again something tugged at him. He went alone this time. He guided a transport truck for the next twenty-five years. Like the Dan River, Saucy flowed from his source to where he emptied into the sea of life. But he always returned.

Saucy's tales from the Depression were entertaining, humorous, often exciting. Yet, they all had a common denominator--Saucy never became all he was capable of becoming. My conclusion about this tragedy, even way back then, was that Saucy's lack of education held him back. I wasn't going to make the same mistake Saucy made.

CHAPTER TWO
BURTON GROVE MEMORIAL STADIUM DAYS

"She made us want to go where the pomegranates grow!" This is how I summed up Mrs. Shoe's contribution to my public school education. I told this to Professor Palmstone of the university's Education Department when Professor Palmstone spoke to the members of Deep South Writing Project who had gathered to learn all they could about the teaching of writing. I was one of twenty-five "writing" teachers who had given up three weeks of summer vacation for a chance to save western civilization. Have you noticed that everybody wants to save western civilization these days, Ronald Reagan, Mortimer Adler, even old Walter Mondale. What's got into these guys? Haven't they read Jeremy Rifkin's *Entropy* or, better still, Oswald Spengler's *Decline of the West* (be sure to give the German title if you want to impress). It's all been said before. Even "It's all been said before," has been said before. It's all Greek to me!

Professor Palmstone was a frenetic man who looked as though he was really interested in my explanation of Mrs. Shoe's methods. Palmstone was interested in teaching methods; his book was testament to his interest.

"Mrs. Shoe was energetic, she was creative, she dared to be different," I told the good professor. He made notes. Then he asked me to write a character sketch of Mrs. Shoe. He said he would include it in an anthology. I haven't heard anything from Palmstone in two years. Has he published the anthology? Was he lying? Was he a blowhard? Was he a Space Cadet?

Burton Grove was an old school when I was a student there. It was a red-brick, single-story structure at the top of Hill Street, just up the hill from the Leaksville Boys' Club. My father went through six grades at Burton Grove. My older brother and older sister both went to B.G. for their elementary school indoctrination. My mother attended Stoneville School in Stoneville, North Carolina, about nine miles west of Leaksville. She still claims she had a better education after six years at Stoneville. Who knows? I was a third generation Burton Grover.

Burton Grove Elementary had a few good teachers (I suppose the principal put out a sign like the Marines: Burton Grove wants a Few Good Teachers!)--teachers who dared to be different, to really teach, to inspire, to be Pygmalions in the classroom. Mrs. Abercrombie was one such teacher. She motivated me to learn. She showed me why learning was important. She had shown my father the same thing. Mrs. Abercrombie worked at her craft. Paideia Proposal to the contrary, Mrs. Abercrombie gave of herself and her time.

After school, she made herself available to students who needed her help. During class, she gave spirited assignments. Yes, she made learning fun.

Mrs. Shoe was even better. Mrs. Shoe taught us everything. Nothing was beyond the scope of Mrs. Shoe's class. I learned to write better , to read better, and to socialize better. Mrs. Shoe was wonderful. Whenever some of us needed to talk, she was willing. If we ever forgot and got "bigger than our breeches," she helped us to make them fit. Occasionally we forgot.

When we studied the Middle East, Mrs. Shoe brought in pomegranates for everyone. Reading about them was interesting, but to taste the tart fruit was a real experience. We tasted what bedouins tasted. She made us want to go where the pomegranates grow.

We made experiments--Pacho Hance and I were reponsible for making a real live volcano. When we made the volcano erupt during open house, we were a big hit. I suppose Mrs. Shoe knew a great deal about what motivates people. Being successful, feeling good about yourself, and being challenged were three feelings I like to experience. Mrs. Shoe made sure we all felt them, and often.

Academic learning did not receive all of her attention. Frankly, I learned to chew with my mouth closed in Mrs. Shoe's class--or, I should say, because she elected to eat lunch with us. She even taught at lunch.

School with Mrs. Shoe was exciting. School did not end when it was out. The world was our school. When Mrs. Shoe had us put together wildflower booklets, she motivated us with the incentive of acquiring numerous wildflowers. I spent many pleasant hours in the woods of Leaksville, near the Leaksville Water Works, searching for Dutchman's Breeches and Mayflowers. I even transplanted one Mayflower to my parents' house and today, I am reminded of my wildflower expedition (and of Mrs. Shoe) when I visist my parents in spring and see the Mayflower blooming. I left the sixth grade feeling good about teachers, myself, and school. Would my junior high teachers and high school teachers be like Mrs. Shoe? This thought more than occasionally filled my head during the summer between the sixth and seventh grades.

CHAPTER THREE
L.S.J.H. DAYS

"May I have your attention please?" Mr. Kirks said solemnly. I held my breath. Mrs. Chipdale stopped scribbling on the board.

"The president is dead," he said icily and with the sound of finality in his voice. We'll never forget that November 22, 1963. That day had a particular feel for me. Three years earlier, my friend Mickey Granger and I, sagacious sixth graders, had ridden a chartered bus from Leaksville--we had caught the bus in front of Cecil's Lunch downtown--to the Greensboro-High Point Airport. We waited in the cold air of October 1960, as the silver jet taxied up to the platform. The door opened. Out stepped a man too youthful-looking to run for the presidency. John F. Kennedy made a quick campaign speech and then worked the crowd. Mickey and I struggled through the crowd and managed, finally, to shake the hand of the great man.

Vivid moments have a way of haunting the present. Some school years, or particular events, or certain moments have a way of lingering over time. I return to them periodically. I spent 1961-1964 at Leaksville-Spray Junior High School. I am still considering the relative merits of those years. I mean, I already knew how to read and write. What did I learn in junior high school? Can anything ever be learned in junior high school? One university colleague has said: "I don't really know what kids, aged eleven to fourteen, should be doing, but I do know that they shouldn't be in school." What was I doing during those L.S.J.H. days?

When I think back on my educational experiences at L.S.J.H., I see what my friend the professor was talking about. Besides the fact that assassins kill presidents, I learned three other things between 1961 and 1964:
- (1) junior high teachers don't ask students to write
- (2) who the Beatles were
- (3) sometimes G.T. (Gifted and Talented) students don't win

Some elaboration is necessary.

There was no Mrs. Shoe or even Mrs. Abercrombie in L.S.J.H.

Mr. Good, bless his soul, helped to destroy our love of literature by making us copy "The Raven" by Poe over and over as a means of punishment. Mrs. Petey had no obvious business teaching algebra. She was oblivious to what was going on in class, algebra or highjinks. Larry and Leonard Neutron, the impish twins, blitzed her chalkboard with watery, gooey spitballs yet she never knew how they got there. She would pull the map or algebraic tables charts down and without fail, a hardened glob of paper would be pocked on the shiny surface.

Only one teacher asked us to write in junior high school. I know you're going to say, "Aw, he's just trying to place blame of his own failures on his teachers." Well, I am--some of my biggest failures were at least partially the fault of my teachers. That was my biggest gripe. It wasn't my only gripe, however.

Seventh grade was spent doing all those things kids have nightmares about: disciplinary procedures, drilling, drilling and more drilling in syntax and grammar. I had dreams about Mrs. Elijah making me copy and recopy spelling definitions until my arms became as hard as a statue's until I looked like the Winged Victory of Samothrace. If you've ever seen the segment of the television series "The Paper Chase" in which first-year law student James Hart has a nightmare where the brutal Professor Kingsfield is strangling him, you have an idea of what I'm talking about. Yet, unlike Professor Kingsfield, Mrs. Elijah and most of her colleagues never assigned us scavenger hunts like Kingsfield did his legal charges. Neither were we asked to role-play like Kingsfield's students. I mean, I realize that every teacher cannot be like Professor Kingsfield, but they can be creative every now and then. Needless to say, there weren't many Space Cadets at L.S.J.H.S.

"Good," you say.

"Bad," I say. Space Cadets are necessary to inspire, to irritate, to challenge, to madden, to revitalize, to create, to live on other planets--to educate!

More often than not, writing was used as punishment. Mr. White Bucks, a throwback to the Pat Boone era, was very good at using

14

writing as punishment. Many of my fellow students and I--some were Space Cadets even then--deserved punishment for pranks, obnoxious behavior, and the like; but, using writing as punishment probably killed more than one writing talent. What a great memorial to a teacher: that he/she killed the most writing talent in the whole junior high school. How would you like to be thought of as "most likely to destroy creativity"? Mr. White Bucks, who always wore khaki pants and sleeveless sweaters (and his white bucks, of course), had greasy hair parted on the right. Was he right-brained? He wasn't malicious. He even meant well--I think! He was just not a writer and he was not a teacher of writing. There aren't that many Donald Murrays around, anyway. Murray's *A Writer Teaches Writing*, published way back there in the dark ages of 1968, is a timeless piece that should be in the hands of every aspiring (and perspiring) teacher.

White Bucks would make us copy all of "The Raven" for almost any infraction in school. If we were late for class, if we talked too much, if we failed to hand in homework, he would say, "You will copy 'The Raven' after school." The only time that I can recall his offering an alternate choice of punishments was when three fellow students (the spit-ball throwing Neutron twins and Gorgeous George) and I dived into the floor at the beginning of English class and looking to the heavens, yelled in unison, "The birds! The birds!" Numerous copies of the "The Raven" and multiple viewings of Hitchcock's "The Birds" had helped us formulate creative madness. We were marched to the principal's office and made to report after school for work details every day for two weeks.

Mr. White Bucks was only one teacher who didn't invite us to write. Many of his colleagues fell into this same non-writing (maybe non-teaching is a useful synonym here) category. Yet, as there had been Mrs. Shoe in elementary school, there was Miss Paideia in junior high school. She wasn't quite so dynamic as Mrs. Shoe, but she was a Space Cadet. And, as I've emphasized, that ain't . . . uh . . . isn't all bad! How could I make fourteen on my verb conjugation test and rave about Miss Paideia's teaching ability? She asked us to write and to play! As that famed Dutch medievalist, Johan Huizinga,

15

articulated in his classic Homo Ludens, "play is at the basis of culture." Whoever forgets (or whoever has not learned) about play forgets about teaching (and about being human). Miss P. was no athlete, but she knew about play. She knew about what George Leonard wrote about in The Ultimate Athlete: the dance inside the game.

Miss Paideia, I mean Miss P., believed in producting well-rounded scholars. She encouraged athletics and was even the cheerleading sponsor. In 8th grade English class, she wanted us to take part in our own education. How nice, you say. How can a student become truly educated if he is never allowed to perform in his own educational theatre? Never fear to lecture to students at any level, but give them a balanced diet of lecture, discussion, role playing, planning, and other varieties of teaching techniques. Exploring in the woods or in the library can broaden the mind much better than being brow-beaten with cribbed lecture notes and the "purple plague," the constant diet of mimeographed sheets on which the students must write, to the nth degree, the answers to questions sometimes not directly related to the purpose at hand.

Miss Paideia wanted to cause a change in us (with a name like Paideia, what else would you expect?). Part of the change in us was affected by role-playing.

I read James Michener's Bridges at Toko-Ri that year and it mesmerized me. I got a chance to strut my stuff. It was "playing army" all over again. I had commanded companies of pretend soldiers for as long as I could remember. When my nephews and friends weren't around to serve as colonial militia, the army of Northern Virginia, Caesar's legions, the 82nd Airborne, or William The Conqueror's tenants-in-chief, I commanded imaginary troops. Miss P. must have known this. Miss P. had no little brothers, but she knew enough about child psychology to let us work with what we knew.

Miss P. divided us into groups of eight and assigned us the task of turning Bridges at Toko-Ri into a play. In my group I begged to play the part of Harry Brubaker, the thoughtful pilot who was torn between serving his country and his desire to be with his family (you remember William Holden in the movie version). Petey Clark played the Mickey Rooney part — he even had a green top hat like Mickey's, and he wore a muffler. In the movie version, Mickey Rooney was a hard-drinking, hard-loving, hard-luck helicopter pilot. Mickey Erby played "Beer Barrell," another hard-drinking man who was responsible for bringing the fighter planes down safely on the floating target that was the aircraft carrier.

Our play was so good that we were dubbed "Best." We were asked to perform it for the rest of the class. Even the class knew it was good. And why not? We were doing what we knew--playing, acting, strutting our stuff. Miss Paideia knew that. She did not fear it. She tapped the almost extra-terrestrial energy of fourteen year-old boys and girls.

Her piecé de resistance, as far as most of us were concerned, was our "field trip" to the Greensboro Coliseum to see a New York touring company's production of "My Fair Lady." We were stunned. All of a sudden there was us right in front of our eyes. The whole class rode a chartered bus to Greensboro, forty miles from L.S.D. (Leaksville, Spray, Draper, North Carolina). On the way, young romance was in the air (many of Miss P.'s students liked that aspect of the trip also). My young lady and I talked and talked all the way to Greensboro. I was too shy to even hold her hand on the way over. But after seeing Liza Doolittle's transformation (and Professor Higgins' transformation), I managed to hold her hand on the way back. Another transformation was beginning.

We still talk about our trip to Greensboro to see "My Fair Lady." It was the greatest academic or cultural trip in all twelve years of public schools. It ranks somewhere up there with my trip to Durham, North Carolina as a member of the high school basketball team in 1966--a trip that ended with our winning the state championship that year. It opened our eyes about musicals, about communication, about creativity, more than a billion mimeographed sheets could ever do! Thank you, Miss P., Space Cadet. Thanks for making us write and helping us learn.

Gifted and talented students don't always win. They may even

17

burn out before they reach college. The G.T. gang (known in some circles as academically talented, academically gifted, smart-alecks, hot-shots — sometimes shot is spelled with an i) was referred to as Academically Talented when I was in junior high in L.S.D.

I had made all As in sixth grade under Mrs. Shoe but, all of a sudden, I found myself in the almost G.T. class. I asked myself why. "How can Jean Wart and Merlin Mitchell be in Academically Talented class and not me?" "Hadn't I created that volcano in sixth grade?" What have they got that I don't have? My two answers were these:

      (1)   Daddies with dollars
      (2)   good behavior.

Yeah, I really believed (and still believe) that the dollar Daddies, who wield clout in little towns like James Coburn wields an American Express card, persuade teachers, principals (always remember, the principal is your pal--if you believe that, I've got some oceanfront property in Illinois I'd like to sell you) and administrators to place their children into academically advanced classes whether they belong there or not. That's very genetic thinking, isn't it? Daddy's got a lotta dough, president of the Kiwanis, country-clubber, works for the athletic boosters at the high school, steady churchgoer, has a gigantic mortgaged home, a Mercedes, maybe a Cadillac for family trips, rancho deluxe, so why not Junior? Daddy must have a lot of brains to acquire all that merchandise. So, junior must have a lot of brains too. Junior's cute like Daddy, must be a smart little chip off the old block-head. Bet he can play sports, too. Dad could. Who said feudalism was dead? Primogeniture, patronage and tribal ceremony are alive and well in small Southern towns. Maybe feudal sons aren't Space Cadets, what do you think? Frederick II of Hohenstaufen was certainly a Space Cadet, wasn't he? He was a Space Cadet educator as a matter of fact. He wanted to see if an infant could develop normal human traits if it did not come into contact with other humans. He placed the child in a barrel and had his scribes observe the responses. The child died. Cruel. Wouldn't it take a Space Cadet to dream up such an experiment in the thirteenth century? I don't know.

I've often wondered if that same Frederician philosophy isn't behind public education. School is a place where students are placed without the benefit of human adult contact for six to eight hours a day. At any rate, Frederick was the Holy Roman Emperor so he didn't need his tort insurance. Without being too sarcastic and insensitive, I wonder how many teachers, including me, have "killed" students academically with their tired and worn out methods and their use of the "purple plague" and other educational torture devices. No, it doesn't sound medieval. Frederick II could just as easily have said, "Sounds Modern, doesn't it?"

Frederick II of Hohenstaufen was one academically-talented kid with money who would have been properly placed if he had been in a G.T. class. So would Eleanor of Aquitaine. But, if she had lived in L.S.D. and had attended L.S.J.H., she would have been refused entry into the Academically Talented class because she would have been thought too rambunctious. The school-based committee, with their eyes ever on community morality, would have shuddered at Eleanor's bare-breasted ride through the streets of Jerusalem on the Second Crusade. So what if she wrote excellent courtly love lyrics? Probably would invite progressive displays of affection--right in the halls! Nope, Eleanor would have been placed in the regular classroom, whatever that is/was (no constipated students in there, I have you know), to be "killed" by some B.S. in education major with a concentration in social studies. No Space Cadets for us, please!

I missed out on one of my junior high school's greatest teachers by having no Daddy with dollars and not very good behavior. I wasn't that bad behaviorally, but I talked all the time. I finished my work before anyone else in class and then disturbed the students sitting near me. The school-based committee, which did not include a psychologist way back there in the "Dark Ages" of 1962, decided that I did not belong in the Academically Talented class. Therefore, I never was taught by noted Space Cadet Rutherford Reynard Bielsky. R.R. Bielsky was a Space Cadet of the first rank--eccentric, demanding, strange, articulate, learned. Isn't it strange how the feudal guys, who seem to cringe at Space Cadetism, really want learned Space Cadets teaching their children? Step'n'Fetchits and Space Cadets are perceived as basically the same by the feudal lords of small Southern towns. So, rather than the stimulating stuff of Rutherford Reynard Bielsky, I ended up on the medieval rack of sequential, dull and void pedagogy. I've since looked back at the vitae of my junior high teachers: not a master's degree among'um.

But, G.T.'s (or, A.T.'s) don't always win! Take the organized debate between the G.T. class and Mr. Meaney's dunderhead class. It was the Spring of 1964, "She Loves You" was in the air, and Mr. Meaney had weathered the winter of his discontent with us, maybe his most disordered civics class. The G.T. civics class proposed a debate with four of our charges in Mr. Meaney's class. We accepted the challenge. I along with Petey Clark, Phil Deal, and Neil Ruthless, were chosen to lock intellectual horns with four G.T. students: Lewis Mills, Mike Raynor, Bobby Spareus, and Gerald Trojan--four of the most brilliant minds in school.

We crammed, researched, crammed. "Should the U.S. Sell Wheat to Russia?" was the resolve. I can't remember who was affirmative and who was negative. But, as you've already guessed by my priggish enthusiasm, I remember who won. What a victory! The Space Cadets defeated the Brief Case Carriers (Brief Case Carrier is long for pointy heads). We did it with hard work, dedication, and confidence in ourselves. They thought they had it wrapped up from the beginning. They didn't.

I grew up with the Beatles in junior high. They appeared one dark and stormy night in February of 1964 (thanks to Mr. Bulwer-Lytton for the setting of this night) on the Ed Sullivan show. The previous fall, as I entered the ninth grade, we all were beginning to hear about the four rock'n'roll musicians from England. The more we heard their records, the more we liked them. We were so carried away that four friends and I decided that we wanted to form a band like the Beatles. We were the first in our neighborhoods to purchase Beatle wigs. Talk about getting second and third looks! One night in February 1964, I attended a high school basketball game. I tried to get through the door sporting my new Beatle wig. Mr. Hendrix, who prided himself on his Prussianism and his management of the

20

system's school buses, asked me to step out of line. He said, in rather intimidating fashion, that I could not enter the gym dressed in my new hair. I asked why. That was all he needed. I was told to leave, wig and all. No reason was given. I suppose he had to protect the community from Space Cadets like me.

I'm sure that I learned something about Space Cadets from the Beatles. How could I help learning from them? I played the radio continuously. My first album by the Beatles was "Meet the Beatles." John Lennon became a hero to take his place in my pantheon of heroes: Art Heyman, the Duke basketball All-American, Johnny Unitas, the Polish football star with the Baltimore Colts, and other great Americans and Europeans.

Lennon's role model for me was both daring and dangerous. He and his three colleagues seemed innocent enough (my mother liked Paul McCartney best) but they obviously were a threat to certain traditions. All of a sudden, learning to play guitar and sing rock'n'roll lyrics took its place alongside learning to block, tackle, hit high hard ones, and shoot layups with either hand.

My civics teacher, the one who had encouraged the Space Cadets to do battle with the Brief Case Carriers, was not a Space Cadet himself. He thought that his M.Ed. from the University of North Carolina at Chapel Hill gave him educational license, but this man was no poet. His training on "the Hill" did not prepare him for the shockwave produced by Beatlemania. I remember his rather innocuous explanation when he said that the Beatles played the following sounds: Va,Va, Voom. According to our brilliant rock musicologist, John would have struck the note for Va, Paul the next Va, and George the Voom. Ringo, according to this scheme, would have banged his Ludwigs in some sort of time. Mr. Mainstay was not plugged into innovative ideas. They may be thirty-five, forty, sixty, or past retirement, but they have a zest to know, to keep up, to impress their students and their peers with their knowledge. Space Cadets are intellectually and culturally alive.

The Beatles' lyrics provided many boys at L.S.J.H. with the romantic words and ideas that they needed to step into the world of wooing (Thomas Moore, the English Romantic poet, would have been proud of the "Time They Lost in Wooing"). They listened when the Beatles told them that "She Loves You" and they were encouraged to "Hold Her Hand." Mr. Mainstay could not grasp this. The fires of love had burned out in him long ago. The fires of love were just beginning to ignite in a young Space Cadet like me. I was already on Mars and I had not left Leaksville.

CHAPTER FOUR
WHAT PRICE HIGH SCHOOL?

If junior high was relatively uninspiring for a budding Space Cadet, high school was an unmitigated bore--academically, that is. Except for Mrs. Shoe. You thought we left her in elementary school. We did but she wouldn't stay. Lucky for me!

Mrs. Shoe took a leave of absence after having her first and only son. After her child was old enough to be left with a sitter, she taught in elementary school. Mrs. Shoe decided to go back to high school teaching, her first love. In fact, she had been a high school teacher most of her career. She was a living example that a Space Cadet...er...good teacher can teach at any level. A Space Cadet can take an educational idea and adapt it to any educational situation. To put it another way, a student in high school social studies class should not have to refer to Reader's Digest to learn about Darwinism.

I was in Mrs. Shoe's biology class in high school. Just as in elementary school, she gave us creative scientific experiments. No, not just cutting the worm, everybody does that. The state department supplies big, ugly earthworms so that at least every biology teacher will appear to be creative at least once a year. But Mrs. Shoe encouraged us to challenge ourselves and to be the best we could be. Isn't that good teaching? That woman was a real Space Cadet! Like John Lennon, Frederick II of Hohenstaufen, Thomas Carlyle, and others, she mixed her ideas well. She instilled in us a desire to understand the world around us.

Yet, the reprise of Mrs. Shoe was about it for my high school education. And, I had her biology course in tenth grade! But, I warned you at the beginning that high school was an academic bore. But, thank goodness, there are other spheres of life about which young people must learn. Athletics, for example, provided some excitement and some meaning. We won a conference football championship during my tenth grade year. Although I broke my collarbone, football proved to be a good diversion. Basketball was even better! Another space cadet, Giles Luney and I played guards on the junior varsity team. Giles was a real Space Cadet.

23

Teachers and parents will do anything for kids--to a limit! I remember one of my teachers, Mr. Harrison, who was also a baseball coach. He was a studious looking, mild-mannered Clark Kent type who, unfortunately, owned no capes. Yet, he was A-okay! I remember the day the guys on the varsity baseball team hid his car. We laughed like crazed hyenas! Finally, we told him that we had pushed it behind the technical-vocational building. He didn't get angry at all! I--we--were amazed. He did all right, that Mr. Harrison.

Giles Luney--we sometimes called him Luney Tunes--was a goofy guy (you might say he was in the wild and crazy mold). He made us all laugh a lot. He got hurt in the tenth grade and had to have false teeth--Yuck! I remember it well. It was over the Christmas holidays. Luney and some of his friends were sledding and he smashed into a car like a torpedo making a direct hit. The crash mangled his nose and mouth; he got up stunned, spitting teeth like an Angelfish firing at its prey.

Although he was through for the year in basketball, Giles usually spent a great deal of time at the Leaksville Boys' Club (like the rest of the guys). His new false teeth even became a prop in Luney's most well-known character, the Sun Demon. Whenever a mischievous mood came over Luney, he would pull his pants up under his arms, poke out his belly, let his false teeth slide half-way out of his mouth so that he could stick his tongue out of the top of his upper plate, and bellow a strange noise: "Subba-Dubba!" "Subba-Dubba!" "Subba-Dubba!" The older boys thought Luney was actually looney. The younger boys were generally afraid. Take rolly-poly Roy "the Boy" Cantor, as an example. Roy would come waddling into the Boys' Club with his homemade basketball jersey (he usually had misspelled Duke to read Duck, with the number 25 below the misspelling).

Seeing a fat kid with Duck/25 on his shirt automatically got the attention of the Sun Demon. Luney would step into the shadows near the front door of the club, silently make the transformation from Giles Luney into the hideous creature and finally lunge out at Roy Cantor, yelling "Subba-Dubba!" "Subba-Dubba!" The Sun Demon would chase the rotund Cantor round and round the table tennis tables with Cantor puffing like a freight train until the Boys' Club manager arrived upon the scene to exorcise the devilish fiend, much like Peter Cushing doing his handiwork on Christopher Lee (you remember, Dr. van Helsig and Count Dracula). The exorcism usually lasted about a week--the length of time Luney was expelled from the club.

A week later he'd be back. Henry the straight man would begin. Then, from behind a dark hallway stepped the Sun Demon screaming, hissing, and subba-dubbaing all over the place.

Luney survived the sledding accident. He was out of basketball for a while, but he lived to do both again. His greatest Subba-Dubba triumph came when we were in the eleventh grade (1965-66). We had just won the North Carolina State IIIA Championship in basketball. We all were yelling and whooping it up in the locker room. The Sun Demon struck!

Mr. Harrison, who also doubled as assistant baseketball coach, was celebrating in his own quiet, out-of-the-way manner. From behind a locker door, that fiend appeared--like a Grendel looking menacingly at an unarmored Beowulf. As the half-smiling, helpless-looking Mr. Harrison looked on, the Sun Demon bellowed his blood-curdling cry, "Subba-Dubba"!

Little did the Sun Demon know that this was his death knell. Like a sphinx who has just had its riddle solved, the Sun Demon perished as Mr. Harrison, for the first time as a teacher, fired some humanity at the Sun Demon. Mr. Harrison pulled his pants up under his armpits, bent over like the lad from Notre Dame, looked menacingly, and grunted, "Subba-Dubba!" "Subba-Dubba!"

We laughed bodily! The Sun Demon died like the sphinx. I usually don't think about this incident, but when I do, I have to grin. I usually think about the Sun Demon and Mr. Harrison and all those ridiculously human high school things whenever I hear someone say, "Subba-Dubba!"

Coach Quigg, the assistant football coach, would qualify for a designation as a "Semi-Space Cadet." If he had had a positive attitude, he would have received a higher S.C. rating. He was eccentric enough, but his brutality and abuse of players and students make me put him out of the S.C. echelons.

Quigg loved to make high school football players feel stupid. He intimidated anyone he could any time he could. When I ran a play incorrectly (I was the quarterback), he would flog my head with his baseball cap and tell me how dumb I was. See I can't exactly put Coach Quigg in the Space Cadet pantheon, now can I? Can you blame me?

My eleventh grade year was probably my worst ever. We were one win and nine losses in football (which, after opposing coaches found out that we had an ineligible player on the team, became 0 and 10!). The football team was a disaster, an unparalleled disaster (some critics of interscholastic athletics feel that all athletics are disasters--I can't agree). But, there were two memorable Space Cadets on the football team, Duffy Wiz and Stevie Hoover. Duffy was the first-string Q.B. when he was a senior and I was a junior. Stevie was the tight end. Their chief claim to Space Cadetism came in the last game of the season. With a record of one win and eight losses, there was little motivation to win it for the Gipper, or anyone else for that matter! Most of the twenty-five survivors (out of the 100 that suited up for the first game) only hoped that they could make it through the last game free of injury. Duffy's and Hoover's antics kept everyone's spirits high--even mine, even with my right ankle in a cast. Even when the score escalated to twenty-eight-zip (that's twenty-eight to nothing in football talk), Duffy had them laughing in the huddle (and, Leonard Cohen's Beautiful Losers had not even appeared in 1965).

Duffy tossed the playbook out. He made up plays as the game progressed (or, regressed, from our perspective): "Hot tuna on second hut," "get down, baby, on first hut," and "see ya later, alligator" were only some of the infamous plays that he called. All of them had a common theme: Hoover and the wide receiver, Petey, would run for the end zone like discount-hounds at a loss of lease sale and wait for Duffy's spiral to land. Such a dazzling repertoire resulted in a 42-8 licking for our season finale. I was almost glad I had a broken ankle and therefore believed that I did not have to take the blame for such a calamity. There was always next year.

The disastrous football season ended, to everyone's relief. Basketball season began! Things had to improve. My broken ankle, which had made me one of the seventy-odd football casualties, forced me to report late for practice. When I did get to basketball practice, the season was five games old.

Basketball was the opposite of football that year. As Jason Miller has so aptly depicted in his play, for us 1966 was "That Championship Season." We stormed through the regular season. The Tobacco Worms, our chief rivals, gave us hard games three times, but we prevailed.

The finest hour came in the Jack Tar Hotel in downtown Durham, North Carolina. The fifteen-man basketball team checked out of school for three days and lived luxuriously in the Jack Tar. We were seeded number one.

Space Cadet Duffy Wiz, the seventh man, performed creatively off the court as well as on. His first antic was to hide a fifth of Smirnoff Vodka in the heating vent. His piecé de resistance was on Friday afternoon, the afternoon before the semifinals and our victory over Durham Jordan High School.

Duffy got David Sykes and me (we had the distinction of rooming with Duff) to cover him with shaving cream. Duff stripped to his jockey shorts and we three emptied numerous cans of Noxema. Finally, we had Duff looking like the Abominable Snowman. Two young women were the first to behold this walking snowdrift, this mobile objet d'art. The house detective, unfortunately, was the third. In a rather stern voice, Duff was told to get back in his room. He did.

Antics like these advanced the cause of Space Cadetism and salvaged some sweet moments from my eleventh grade year. If only more of the teachers could have been like Duffy Wiz.

Needless to say, there were few Space Cadets among my high school teachers. Quigg was my algebra teacher--uninspiring. My Spanish teacher was in her first, and hopefully, her last year. Because of her, I let my Spanish fly out the window. Saul Sheppard, my eleventh grade chemistry teacher, spent too much time in his lab office adjacent to the chemistry lab. I often wondered what he spent his time doing in there. I later found out that he was taking indecent liberties with his female lab assistant. While I struggled to find the "unknown" in my vial, that vile fellow was leaving nothing to the imagination. I suppose scientists are like that. My eleventh grade English teacher, Mrs. Tradition, was real close to being a Space Cadet. She followed her own instincts usually in opposition to her colleagues. To be a real Space Cadet, you've got to wear those out of style clothes (or, those really in-style clothes) in style!

The only Space Cadet I had for a teacher in the eleventh grade was Mr. Brucie (we called him Cousin Brucie after the famous WBZ-Boston disc jockey of the sixties). Brucie was almost Mrs. Shoe. He made us expand our horizons and detested our provincialism. He gave us year-long assignments of studying individual countries, collecting data, and then unloading the data in front of the class in May. I chose Germany. Brucie occasionally spoke German in class. His geography class focused on Europe even though we also studied extra-European affairs. Geography is notoriously dull for middle and high school students, particularly if the teacher is un-creative and assigns chapter after chapter of reading and then begins an epidemic of the purple plague. Mr. Brucie didn't teach that way. He was a Pygmalion in the classroom. He loaded us up with work and expected a great deal from us. We griped about the work, but we were glad for what he taught us. And, that he taught us to learn!

Mr. Brucie integrated music, art, and culture into his geography lessons. Like Mrs. Shoe, he made us want to go where the pomegranates grow (or the strudel, bangers and mash, and truffles). I trace my real interest in European history to my older brother Richard (a history major) and to Mr. Brucie.

I think Mr. Brucie left our high school because he was a Space Cadet. He knew that he needed to fly to another educational planet, to find other beings like himself. He did just that. Mr. Brucie, the last time I heard from him, was pursuing a Ph.D. in Middle Eastern

Studies at a well-known midwestern university. He probably found other Space Cadets there.

I was fortunate to have a positive teacher model like Mr. Brucie. Thanks, Mr. Brucie (and Mrs. Shoe, Mrs. Paideia, etc.)

Athletics had saved me in the tenth and eleventh grades. Rock music was to provide some stability and spice throughout my high school sojourn.

I can hear Ed Sullivan now in his ultra-dry, deadpan way: "Now, here they are, The Beatles!" We were mesmerized. They grinned boyishly. Even the long hair could not detract from their basic wholesomeness and the positive energy they emitted. Even my mother had to admit she kinda liked them. She liked Paul the best (the "cute" Beatle). Paul shouted, "one, two, three, bop," and they were off into "I Saw Her Standing There." To my friends and me, a revolution had begun. We were fourteen and ready to join in. I neither knew nor cared that advance men for the Beatles had covered the United States with a blitz of Beatle records and paraphernalia to whip the masses into a Beatle frenzy. Ross didn't care, either. He was my friend and we determined then and there that the Beatles were for us.

Ross and I were never the same after the Beatles exploded upon the American music scene. We knew we had to play music. "Let's get a guitar and amplifier for Christmas and form a band," one of us suggested to the other. "Righto!" the other retorted.

That Christmas, Ross got a black and white Silvertone guitar and amp. My football injury provided me with enough insurance money to invest in a Gibson SG-Standard and a small Gibson amp. There I was with a first-rate guitar and a no-rate ability. "What am I gonna do with this thing? I asked Ross. "Play it!" he said. "O.K.," I said. So, the band was born in December of 1964. The fact that we could not play our instruments was looked upon as only a temporary roadblock. We were fourteen and full of energy.

"Who'll drum for us?" I asked Ross. "That's a good question," Ross Responded. We began the search for a drummer. Everyone seemed to have gotten a set of Sears drums for Christmas - but we wanted someone who could play. My cousin, Butch, got a few drums (not a complete trap set, of course). He agreed to let my friend, Mot Feldon, play them. Mot was known, among other things, for his ability to keep time to the music on the radio at the Boys' Club.

Needless to say, our first performance was a total wipeout (we even played "Wipeout" by the Safaris). I played the Gibson, Ross twanged the Silvertone, and Mot thumped a beat on Butch's drum kit. We played "I'm a Loser" by the Beatles and "Long Tall Texan," a hayshaking, semi-rockabilly, sub-Jerry Lee Lewis noise. Our terrible playing was in disproportionate relationship to the crowd's musical naivete. We were, however, the first in the neighborhood to go the Beatle route. Even Mickey Granger exclaimed, "You guys sure have got guts to play that mess."

"If you ain't got your own material you'll never make it," we were constantly reminded. Most of our critics didn't even know where Liverpool was. But, they were right. No one wanted to hear the Furies, the Rockin' Ramblers, or the Missing Links (all band names of ours) sing the five hundredth rendition of "Louie, Louie" in every one-horse dive from Richmond to Spokane.

Ross and I spent the first year of our band existence going through numerous personnel changes. We labored long and hard trying to mimic the stars like the Beatles, the Searchers, and the Rolling Stones. One of our first polished songs was "Not Fade Away," a Stones' song.

What we needed was a steady band--not to mention steady performances. A steady band was just the thing for our songwriting. We were trying to write what we thought were sixty-ish, Beatle songs. However, the Beatles moved fast. By the time that I had a few songs which resembled the four-chord blues of "Money," "Dizzy Miss Lizzie," and "Bad Boy," the Beatles jumped to feedback, many minors and sharps--I was out of date before I got started.

How we dredged up Chris Crootch as a drummer, I'll never know. I looked behind me one day and he was there sitting behind his red Ludwigs. Chris's parents allowed us to practice at their house. This helped considerably. Chris was the proverbial briefcase-carrying teenager--unathletic, asocial, and snobbish. He was also very pig-headed. If he thought his ideas would carry the day, he'd have to think again. This band belonged to me and my friend Ross.

Soon after Chris became a member of the band, we landed another guitar player, Raleigh Miller. "Ole Rally," as we called him, was as stocky and short as Chris was tall and skinny. We certainly weren't going to win any handsome band contest (but, the Rolling Stones had made it, hadn't they?). Besides, we still needed a bass player. Even though the present personnel helped establish us as a name band in the Leaksville, Spray, and Draper area, the individual members' different ideas about music and the type of music we should play were constant sore spots. Would they one day cause our downfall? Chris and Raleigh loved Soul and Beach music. Ross and I were Folk-rockers from the word go. Somehow, we compromised.

Irony of ironies: Mickey Granger just up and decided one day that he'd like to play bass for us--now we were the Missing Links. Nineteen sixty-six proved to be a good year. Our managers, Reuther Macklin and Brian Epley, got us numerous places to play; they weren't the Ritz, but they paid. The Stoneville Sealtest, the Couples Club in Collinsville, Virginia, the local V.F.W. were some of our haunts. We played and waited for the Big Break.

We thought the annual Morehead High School Talent Show was going to be the great success catapult for us. Our time had surely come. The long hours of practice, the relentless trials of trying to flower in a town of weeds, all that and more was behind us. Morehead Auditorium was certainly not the Greensboro Coliseum, but it was a first-rate gig, we thought.

"What are we going to play?" asked Chris at our first, major pre-Talent Show practice session. "Surely our own stuff!" I shot back. "We don't have time to learn it," was someone's wimpy reply. "The hell we don't" I shot back angrily. "Listen, by God, we're finally getting a chance to show the people who the Missing Links are--and we're not going to blow it!" I reasoned. "Sure, Jon, sure,"

Raleigh said condescendingly. The age-old problem was showing its ugly head again. Both Ross and Mickey were quiet on the subject at first. Neither wanted to choose sides--yet.

Willie Dregs appeared out of nowhere. He was a rather short, but well-built, black student from New York. He became a student at Morehead High School. He was a slick dresser (he looked as though he sang with the Temptations). Another "My Girl" singer, I joked to Raleigh as Dregs moved past us. "Yes, I know," Raleigh said with a grin.

For some reason, we didn't practice for a week. Something was wrong. Ross seemed pre-occupied on the bus ride from Burton Grove Elementary School to Morehead High School. Finally, during the second week before the Talent Show, Ross completely stopped riding the bus. I decided to call Ross.

"Jonathan, I think the other band members want you out and Willie Dregs in," Ross explained this staggering blow to me. "Pink-slipped by a third-rate rock band," I replied trying to hide my concern with bravado. "Are you kiddin' me, Ross?" I asked. "I wish I were," my friend replied. "What are you gonna do for the show?" I asked with concern. "Raleigh, Chris, and Mickey want Willie to sing 'My Girl' and some other Soul numbers," he explained. "Damn, how could those third-rate S.O.B.'s do this to me?" I asked rhetorically. "It was my band in the first place!" I yelled. "You know how the other guys felt," Ross tried to reason. "It's just that people around here like Soul and Beach music and you're too bull-headed to realize it--you're not in New York or L.A., Jon," Ross added. "To hell with the Missing Links--and to hell with you," I yelled to my friend. I slammed the phone down.

I learned a few days later that the band had even changed its name--now it was The Illusions. I suppose they thought it sounded more like a Soul band.

"Oh, you can't do that," John Lennon sang. I thought, that's right, they can't do that. I won't take this thing lying down. I've spent too much time and energy the past three years to pass up the chance to play at Morehead Auditorium in front of 2,000 people.

I didn't know how, or with whom, but I was going to form a new band and perform in that talent show — no matter what! My first thought was to recruit my old friend Gigger Kanter. Gigger and I had known each other since elementary school. As a matter of fact, it had been Gigger, two other guys, and I had who started the Leaksville-Spray, and Draper version of the Beatles at Leaksville-Spray Junior High School in the spring of 1964. Long before the real bands were born--the Furies, the Rockin' Ramblers, the Missing Links, etc.--Gigger, Gary Masters, and Petey Carlyle pretended we were the Beatles for the gang at the junior high school. Why, we even were the first to wear Beatle wigs.

Gigger had not been bitten by the music bug like Ross and me, but he agreed to perform. Yet, we still had only one guitar. Time for more recruits, I told myself. I knew some tenth-grade guys who had recently formed a band called the "Successions." One week before the Talent Show, I went to one of their practice sessions.

"Where's Ross Marion and the other Missing Links?" Ganges Myer, one of the Successions' guitarists inquired. "I hate to say it, but I'm no longer with the Missing Links," I confessed. "You're what?" a stunned Giles Triad asked. "I'd rather not go into details," I said. "Gigger and I came here to ask you guys a favor," I hinted. "How would you like to play in the Morehead Talent Show?" I asked enthusiastically. "Do you think we're good enough?" Ganges asked innocently. "I wouldn't have asked if I had thought otherwise, now would I?" I asked. Yes, I would have. "Sure, we'll play, won't we boys?" Ganges asked the other two. They all three agreed.

"What'll we call ourselves and what'll we sing?" Subba Washburn the bass player asked. "Let's take question two first," I suggested. "I know enough songs for us to get by at the audition," I assured everyone. The younger guys were not in a position to argue. They wanted to play in the Morehead Talent Show. They quickly settled for my folk-rock repertoire. The set included: "Bad to Me," by Billy J. Kramer and the Dakotas (another Beatle-wave band from England and even managed by the Beatles' manager, Brian Epstein); "A

Younger Girl," by the Lovin' Spoonful; "I'll Feel A Whole Lot Better," by the Byrds; and "Don't Throw Your Love Away," by the Searchers. Gigger Kanter had had much shower-singing experience. Plus, Gigger was confident; he knew all the girls would fall at his feet once he cranked up at the Talent Show. With only a few weeks to go, we needed that kind of confidence. The mission seemed quite impossible: here I was with four beginning musicians trying to take on a band (the former Missing Links) that I knew was tighter and . . . better. Nevertheless, we . . . I had to do it. Those guys can't do that to me, I thought.

Monday morning, May 20, 1967, breezed in out of nowhere. When Mickey Granger broke a two-and-a-half week silence, I forgot about the Viet Nam Conflict and the fact I had to be in homeroom in two minutes. "I hear you guys are planning to audition today," Mickey asked snidely. "That's right, we can't let the Links walk away with it," I bragged. "You don't think you have a chance, do you?" Mickey asked. "We'll do all right," I assured him. "I'll say one thing," Mickey said as he continued his stupid grin and shook his head. "What's that?" I asked. "You guys sure have a lot of guts to play that mess!" he said. "Haven't I heard that before?" I asked sarcastically. I turned without saying so long and walked to Mr. Urban's homeroom. Seeing Princess Peony Cherry in homeroom made me forget, for an instant, the painful Talent Show.

When I walked past the tenth grade class of Mrs. Vine, she was giving a boring lecture on parts of speech. I wondered if any English teacher in that school system ever talked about anything except the parts of speech. Giles, Subba, and Ganges were sitting impatiently listening to Mrs. Vine. I motioned for them to fake thirst and get permission to go to the fountain. Somehow, Mrs. Vine was so inebriated by her own rhetoric, that she gave them permission without missing a beat in her presentation of prepositions.

"Listen, you guys, today is it!" I explained urgently. "Mr. Betterman wants us there at 3:15 p.m. sharp!" I continued my sense of urgency. Gigger and I had already talked with Mr. Betterman, and he assured us we'd get a fair shot. Betterman wouldn't keep us out. We kinda liked Betterman. Finally, after some more coaching, I hustled Giles, Ganges, and Subba back to Mrs. Vine's inspirational lecture. I could tell by their nauseated faces that they appreciated it.

Claudia Ginger was putting her robe back on when we pushed open the door to the "Glee Club" room. I almost fell over Betterman's metronome as I was mesmerized by Claudia's dazzle. As Coach Gregory had remarked, "She was too much for one man, and not enough for two."

"O.K., Jon, you guys set up right here," Mr. Betterman directed. The only problem, of course, was the drum kit. Subba finally had it complete. The guitar amps were small and easy to prepare. We plugged our chords into the amps. The loud feed-back startled some of the hangers-on in the crowd.

"O.K.," I said, "'Bad to Me' in C." I cranked out the intro and we were off into a ballad by Lennon/McCartney. We finished the number with only a few rough spots. Betterman was pleasantly surprised. "Why didn't you two try out for the Glee Club?" he asked Gigger and me. "Ah, we knew we couldn't make it," we grimaced.

"Your style will give us a refreshing contrast to the other band's," Betterman explained. The other band, by the way, was the Illusions. "By the way, what do you guys call yourselves?" Betterman asked and pulled out his clipboard. We looked at each other. Finally, I said, "The Studs." "The Studs?" Betterman asked, somewhat in disbelief. "The Studs!" I emphasized. "O.K., it's your band," Betterman agreed.

Saturday, May 25, came sooner than we expected. We managed to practice three times during the week. The crowd hummed as it filed into the auditorium. I was noticeably nervous. The student master of ceremony, Anthony Minnow, had the crowd rolling in the aisles when he said, "The winners will receive one free trip to Tacky Branch." "The losers will receive TWO free trips to Tacky Branch," he added, and the house roared. Frankly, no previous talent show winner had ever amounted to anything. Edith Crabbe, who had dazzled locals with her effortless Mozart, had gone to live in a hippie commune. Carl Hackster, who had wowed them with his virtuoso organ playing, married his male lover three years after his triumph. Nonetheless, winning the local talent show was still the pinnacle for every two-bit piano-playing, guitar-twanging, zit-squeezing teenager in town. One man's exile to Tacky Branch is another man's Nirvana!

Needless to say, we gave it a good shot. We did a fair rendition of the Searchers' "Don't Throw Your Love Away." They actually liked "A Younger Girl" and "I'll Feel a Whole Lot Better." I was pleasantly surprised. We were in Beach Music and Soul Music country. "Bad to Me" was bad to us. It wasn't that bad, but I could sense that the audience was thinking that a little of us went a long way. I needed Klee's "Fish Magic" to help us swim out of the crowd without being seen or interrogated.

Junie Rollie sang next. She was operatic, quasi-sophisticated, pretty good. The audience was impressed. "Baloney!" Ganges whispered.

The Illusions looked like a poor man's Bob Kuban and the In-Men (you don't remember "The Cheater"?). They were odd-sized with Mickey Granger a head taller than the rest and about sixty pounds heavier. Raleigh was a squat, little guitarist. Willie Dregs was garbed in a gypsy-like poncho a la Al Green. He was good. Their rendition of "My Girl" was like every other small town group's rendition of "My Girl." "My Girl" was the redneck's favorite love song much the same as Creedence Clearwater Revival's "Proud Mary" would become the Redneck National Anthem a year later.

The Illusions played some type of idiotic instrumental and then a version of "Night Train." That's all I remember. I think that we were allowed three or four songs each. Though the audience applauded respectfully for us, I could sense that the Illusions would receive a more intense, longer-sustained applause. I was right.

They won. I thought that was grossly unfair. They had callously dismissed me from the band, replaced me, and then won the Talent Show. I was embarrassed and crushed. "Ganges, let's go to Tacky Branch," I suggested. "Let'er rip!" he said.

36

About a week after the debacle at Morehead High School, Ross Marion, my former old friend, called me. "How are the Delusions?" I kidded. "Jon," Ross said, "I've quit!" "I can't take those dives they're booking," he lamented. He sounded serious, apologetic. He related, in what I considered to be a somewhat self-righteous tone that Mickey, Raleigh and Chris were indulging in too much drink and hurrahing for him. That was fine, I thought, but I wanted him to say that he was sorry for kicking me out of the band and then crushing "The Studs" in the Morehead Talent Show. I knew it would be hard for him to do it.

"I'm not surprised," I feigned a little self-righteousness myself. "Those guys didn't realize what they were getting into when they decided to go 'Big-time!'" I continued my sermon.

Ross was serious. He was really apologetic as well for allowing Crooch, Miller and Granger to kick me out of the group. "Why don't we get together and strum a few," I suggested knowing that Ross had given apologizing his best shot. "Sure," he said but he seemed a bit reserved by my ability to forget (Oh, I didn't forget, but I tried hard to forget for that minute).

Ross and I were back where we had started three years before, sitting on my front porch dreaming about two local yokels from Leaksville "making it" in the big-time world of songwriting and pop music. We were that naive, my old friend Ross and I. Maybe being naive was the way to create Taj Mahals, York Minsters and White Albums.

Looking back in time, particularly that time from first grade through twelfth, I see few Space Cadets: one in elementary school, one or two in junior high, one in high school. Out of the approximately forty "teachers" I was exposed to in twelve years, there were only three Space Cadets.

Jim Morrison's "When the Music's Over" was a premonition (not to mention T.S. Elliot's "The Wasteland"). High school ended with a whimper.

CHAPTER FIVE
WHEN I THINK BACK . . .

"When I think back on all the crap I learned in high school, it's a wonder I can think at all," is a well-known crack at public schools by singer/songwriter Paul Simon, formerly of Simon and Garfunkle. I must say that, after my three years in high school, I almost agreed with Mr. Simon. I say almost because I have some reservations. I probably was a slow starter. And Space Cadets across the curriculum have remedied that. I certainly wasn't allowed to "burn out" in secondary school. My high school teachers certainly allowed me to enter college with some rough edges left to smooth; indeed, about a million rough edges. Would there be Space Cadets teaching in college?

My all-time favorite teacher taught me during my freshman year at Oak College, a small, church-affiliated, co-educational college in Piedmont, North Carolina. Professor J. P. Ancient, scholar of English history, was as effective as a teacher as he was in intellectual circles. He was the model young professor, from his tweed, English suits to his refined manners. He was every inch a professor. He remembered my name, and the names of his others students, only a couple of weeks into the semester. When he saw a student outside of class, it was always an affable (and rather British) hello, Mr. So and So. He was a native of Burlington who long ago had succumbed to the British magic.

Professor Ancient had students over for parties, sponsored the history lecture series, and created a mid-term program that sent students to England for a month. He was a Space Cadet, first class.

Ancient made us want to learn. We wanted to be like him. He was a good model. In every situation, he handled himself well.

Professor Ancient had friends in high places. He occasionally brought them to campus. I remember one year he persuaded Professor Bertie Wilkinson, foremost authority on later medieval English constitutional history, to come to Oak College and lecture to his English history students. We sat outside near the administration building in the shade of the large oaks that dominated Oak College. Wasn't that Plato-like? It was like we were reliving the Academy. We were participants in our own education. That's another Space Cadet characteristic. The Space Cadet expects the students to help in their own educations.

Although Professor Ancient was a Tudor/Stuart man, he also taught the course in medieval history. Oak College was a bit too small to maintain a medievalist. However, Ancient was an adequate teacher of medieval history. I finally received Professor Ancient's "Harvard A" in the medieval course. He reserved that accolade for especially outstanding performances. It seemed that Ancient had attended Harvard U. for a couple of summers. He took to it like a Space Cadet to Venus. That was all he needed to go along with his affected Englishness. But, he pulled it off well.

Professor Ancient left Oak a few years after I graduated. He took a position at the prestigious Folger Shakespeare Library in Washington, D.C. That told me that Space Cadetism impressed more than just a few college students.

There was another Space Cadet-type at Oak. His name was Professor Roland Delano, professor of American History. Whereas Professor Ancient was urbane, dynamic, shiny, and the picture of educated youth, Delano was older, tired, but a wonderful soft-spoken, quietly-demanding teacher. I learned from him that you do not have to intimidate students. He taught me the value of caring and about intellectual honesty. When he gave a test, there were no surprises in it, just like Holiday Inn.

In addition to the two Space Cadet history professors, I discovered three other Space Cadets at Oak College: one was the basketball coach, one an English professor, and the other a religion prof.

Coach Billy Million was a fanatic! He whipped his players into shape unmercifully. He could not--would not--tolerate sloppy play or players who would not pay attention.

"Hey, whatta you doing bothering my boy!" he once yelled at an assistant football coach who stopped by basketball practice and was, from Million's point of view, disturbing an injured player that Million had directed to shoot foul shots at the other end of the court from where the other team members were scrimmaging.

"Sorry Coach," the gigantic man said to the wiry, yet gruesome basketball coach.

"President Donaldson has to make an appointment to come to the gymnasium," Melvin Fitzgerald had once told me. Even the president of the college was in awe of a basketball-coaching Space Cadet. Such was the territorial dominance of Coach Million.

Million had forced Nelson Crane, who had hurt himself horseplaying in the dorm, to shoot free throws during practice even though poor Crane had a cast on from his knee to his big toe. Million decided that Crane needed to be more careful, more mature.

When big, six-foot, eight inch Billy Bullins complained to Million about Western College's rough style of play and asked Million what to do, the coach bellowed in characteristic fashion, "Kick him where it hurts." Million had all the answers.

Professor Radford Bilge was a five-star, grand slam Space Cadet. He had a big, red nose, was bespectacled (some would call him a DUFUS, a 1960s term of derision) and was a true flake (a FLAKE is a Space Cadet who is farthest out). Yet, Bilge was a good teacher of American Literature. He prodded, infuriated, tickled, and all the while he read and acted his way through Emily Dickinson, Walt Whitman, Ralph Waldo Emerson, and a host of others. He would forget about the hot radiators in winter and accidentaly sat back against the bulky branding irons. "Owwww!" he would yell and jump as his recitation of "Captain, My Captain" was momentarily interrupted. In spring, the ever-present bumblebees would wander into the English class. Bilge would continue reading Emily Dickinson, but he would keep an eye out for the buzzing bomber. "Those things can sting like crazy!" he blurted out in mid verse. One day he finally gave up on "The American Scholar" and made a vicious swat at the bee. Space Cadets can implant images in your mind whether they mean to or not. Years after you have been in their midst, you will remember streams of ideas that are attached to a buzzing bumblebee, a Mayflower, a pomegranate.

I walked back to the dorm one winter evening in 1968. Even though the temperature was hovering around 30 degrees and ten inches of whiteness covered Oak College, the guys from Braddock Dormitory had their stereo up loud enough to blow the icicles off the Student Union. Eric Clapton, Ginger Baker and Jack Bruce were reprising last year's smash (for the hundredth time this semester):

It's getting near dark/When night close
its tired eyes/I'll soon be with you my
love/To give you my dull surprise. . .

The last time I saw Professor Bilge, a firm, rock-like snowball was speeding directly for his head. I heard he later got a teaching job at a nearby Community Collge after Oak decided his comic brand of Atheism was not suitable for its students. Frankly, I considered myself a religious person (and still do), but I never considered old Bilge a threat to proselytize me. He was a good teacher. That's all I wanted him for--his Atheism was his own business. However, I decided that the snowball must have missed. Some of his students swear that the snowball must have got him.

Going to Oak College was good for me. I basically learned in my twelve years of public schooling to read and to record. Notice I said recording. That's really the only active writing skill I learned--recording. Recording is simply writing out abstract symbols for sounds in life. It involves no thinking, no revising. I never advanced beyond the recording stage of writing in public schools-- maybe no one is supposed to. However, I believe that I began to move past the recording stage by my junior year in college. Luckily, when I got to college, in addition to rock'n'roll, there were Professors Ancient, Delano, Bilge, and Coach Billy Million. They helped me to fulfill myself. One was an excellent model of the sophisticated human being. Another demonstrated the necessity of honesty in teaching. Yet another conveyed toughness, a trait needed by teachers at all levels. The last reminded me always to look to myself for answers. They were in the best tradition of Space Cadets.

After waving goodbye to Carolyn Streak the day of graduation, I said goodbye to Oak College. As Grand Funk Railroad lamented, "I'm getting closer to my home," I felt like I was getting further away from mine, although I may have really been getting closer.

When I left Oak, I also left the 1960s. Almost all of my education had been in the 1960s. Now, I faced the task of teaching in a new decade. The dawning of the Age of Aquarius was the dawn of me, the teacher. What would I tell my first students? Would they like me--maybe even love me as Professor Ancient's students (including me) loved him? Should teachers wish to be loved? Would they eventually show me that I really did not belong in the teaching profession? (Why was I thinking about getting out before I had gotten started?).

Who was I kidding, anyway? The real question was "Would I ever get a chance to practice my newly-acquired skills--would I ever get a job?" This was 1970-71, the gold mine of teaching jobs of the 1950s and 1960s was not abandoned. However, I had learned a great deal about teaching, particularly from a small, interesting group of Space Cadets who had the courage, the true courage, of their own convictions. Would I have the courage of my own convictions? Would I be a Space Cadet?

CHAPTER SIX
TEACHING WHAT I WAS TAUGHT, 1971-1974

"Everytime a door closes, a window opens." I think Jim Impure, a trustworthy insurance man, gave me that advice. He was correct. Jim was sort of a Space Cadet insurance man who worked for Robert E. Lee Life in Norfolk and had begun to climb the twenty-pay ladder of success with Lee National Life. I met Jim when I went to Winding, Virginia, about thirty-five miles west of Portsmouth and Norfolk. Jim's philosophy was dispensed when I told him that my first teaching job was beginning when my first marriage ended:

"And, in the end, the love you take/Is
equal to the love you make."

The end of the Beatles' "Abbey Road" album fizzled and Jim asked me about my marital status. "I don't have any, anymore," I told Jim. Jim was Johnny-on-the-spot to Winding as soon as the list of new teachers reached his desk.

I learned about the Winding teaching job from my older brother Rick. Rick had been like a second father to me. He was seventeen years older--another generation. He had gone to Oak Collge in the mid 1950s after his U.S. Navy stint. One of his Oak buddies had become principal at Winding. A chance reunion revealed their need of a history teacher who wanted to coach. Rick told George Leonard, the principal and his buddy, that his baby brother was ready to embark on his teaching career.

Rick, his son Willie, and I went to Winding, Virginia, in the heat of the mid-July sun. We traveled highway 58, through Danville, Turbeville, Clarksville (home of Roberts' Restaurant), South Hill, Emporia, Franklin (home of the world's strongest smell), and Winding. When we got to Franklin we turned off 58 onto 258 and drove north toward Smithfield (home of one great ham). Winding was about halfway between Franklin and Smithfield.

The Leaksville boy who had only rarely been outside of Rockingham County, North Carolina, was now on the verge of taking a first teaching job 225 miles from home. Could he do it? Whether

I wanted to or not, I had graduated from Oak; my parents and my brother Rick were counting on me. My feet were getting cold, my hands sweating. John Denver's lines,

West Virginia, Mountain Mama,
Take me home, Country Roads . . .

already made me homesick and I thought ahead of the loneliness of seeing Rick and Willie head back for Leaksville. I had to put on my best brave act.

George Leonard and Rick reminisced fondly about high school in the early 1950s. They talked sports, mostly about their near-legendary coach, Renfield Rose. Leonard was only about five feet, five inches tall. Somehow I had trouble believing those heroic tales he told about himself. Rick had simply learned to live with Leonard's tales of grandeur. Rick was a good athlete in high school. He had started at guard on the football team as a sophomore and was a starting pitcher in baseball. Since I was five, Rick had had a tremendous influence on me, particularly a sports influence. He had even taken me to Lees-McRae College and other schools to try out for basketball and football when I was a twelfth-grader at Leaksville. We both thought I still wanted to be involved in athletics. Rick had coached, so I decided I'd give it a shake.

Winding High School gave me an opportunity to practice my skills as teacher and coach. I had to report to practice on 10 August 1971. I was assistant football coach, head jayvee basketball coach, and head baseball coach. That's a heavy load. Thankfully, Principal Leonard gave me only three classes to teach: world history, world geography, and U.S. History. In addition, I had two study halls and a planning period. Like most school systems, Winding looked after its coaches. While the English and math and science teachers slaved away with six courses a day, I had only three. As can be expected, this system is not conducive to good rapport among coaches and teachers.

Luckily, or unluckily depending upon the way you look at it, I stumbled upon three Space Cadets at Winding High School: Principal

Leonard, Coach Rex Murphy, and history/political science teacher Billy Byerly.

Principal Leonard, all things considered, was an innovative force at Winding. He was years ahead of most southeastern schools in implementing behavioral objectives, those artifical monsters that still haunt all teachers. Yet, with all of his innovations, Leonard never forgot about feathering his own nest. He was economically innovative as well as educationally so.

I remember the day that he introduced me to his idea of the Winding Investors' Club. The idea seemed a sound one. Principal Leonard collected monthly investments from school employees who wished to join. For each ten dollar contribution, the investor received a Winding Investors' Club Certificate. Leonard, who could sell snow to an Eskimo or sewing machines to a Singer salesman, had convinced the teachers and other investors that he was investing the money in a sure-fire deal. "Everyone is guaranteed a 10% return on his money," the principal repeated at every meeting. I only knew of meetings from a friend of mine. She had invested and related the meetings' business to me. I never joined the WIC. Leonard, with respect for my older brother Rick, never lured me in. He even discouraged me from joining. That was the give-away. The year I left Winding, Leonard barely escaped across the state line where he still lives on the property he purchased.

As inauspicious an introduction to Principal Leonard as this is, the man was a good teacher and a good administrator. He would have made the Paideia Group proud. He viewed the principal's role as that of head teacher. Even though he efficiently handled administrative responsibilities, he always had time to visit classrooms and he never failed to make pedagogical suggestions. However, there is a negative side to a principal who overdoes the head teacher role. He is always looking over teachers' shoulders. I had to develop schemes for dealing with Leonard's too frequent visits. I did. One particularly effective one worked like this.

After Mr. Leonard had worn out his welcome in my class — by mid-October — I began to involve him in the lesson plan for the

45

day. A bright, quick-witted history major as an undergrad, Leonard couldn't know everything (although he pretended to). If I was in the midst of a lecture, group discussion, or film, I'd always ask Leonard a difficult question that had already stumped the class. "Let's see if Mr. Leonard can help us with our problem, class," I usually suggested and immediately directed everyone's attention to a reddening principal in his regular position in the back of the class.

"This certainly has been a stimulating lesson, Mr. Carter, but I must move on back to the office," Leonard would avoid the question and walk briskly out of class. The students would smile and we would continue.

To appreciate Leonard's real mettle as a teacher (no, as a Space Cadet), I must share with you a story told to me by a former student of Mr. Leonard. This former student is now an outstanding teacher himself. I accidentally had this fellow in a writing institute one summer. The former student wrote this story of Leonard as part of the course requirement. The story goes like this:

I will always remember my seventh grade at Wishingwell School. My teacher, Mr. George Leonard, was a most unusual man. He ordered us around in military fashion, "March-one-two-three-four." Not marching would get one in a lot of trouble.

The classroom was a veritable laboratory. We had a darkroom converted out of a closet. I thought it was very special because I got to develop film with a girl I had a crush on.

In Mr. Leonard's class, a student could bring charges against anyone who bothered him by paying ten cents and bringing the person to trial. However, I can't seem to remember the punishments that were meted out.

That year each student had to write and produce one play. Mr. Leonard also developed a classroom honor roll system: students with all A's could be on the Constitution Committee; students with all A's and B's could be on the Congress Committee.

One day we were talking about chocolate covered ants and all of us wanted to try some. Mr. Leonard said that if we raised the money for them, he would order some. We put our heads together and decided to hold an auction. We raised the money and gave it to Mr. Leonard. When the ants arrived, none of us except Mr. Leonard would try one. He said they were rather nice.

Our final event as a class that year was a party at Mr. Leonard's house. A Union Jack flying in the front yard was the clue as to where we were when we got in the vicinity of Leonard's house. All the boys were in their best suits and the girls looked beautiful in their party dresses. We danced and feasted on grilled steaks. This was the perfect ending to a fun school year. Thanks Mr. Leonard, wherever you are!

Rex Murphy had been the all-time single season scorer at a four-year college in Eastern Virginia. He had gained almost instant fan support when he took his first Winding High School team to the state championship game. The Winding team, short on talent, was brought along slowly by their young knowledgeable coach. They were only 10-11 at season's end. Then, miracle of miracles, they won the conference tournament. Then they took the regionals. All of a sudden, they were opposite the number one seeded team in the state. They didn't win the final game, but they won the hearts of the Winding people. Murphy was an overnight success. His subsequent teams produced much better regular season records, but they never achieved a state championship.

Murphy ranks as a Space Cadet because he was the good teacher/coach. He not only told the students how to throw a good bounce pass, he threw good bounce passes, while dressed as Rudolf Valentino. By the time I came to Winding, still possessed by the desire to coach, Murphy was in his seventh year. He was thirty years old, about five feet, nine inches, with a slight paunch (too many post-game Budweisers). I wondered how this surprisingly short man had amassed nearly 2,000 points as a college basketball player. When we played the boys' basketball team, I found out. He could shoot the eyes out as they say. In practice, he had the ability to demonstrate all phases of the game.

Murphy dared to innovate. He had collected plays from all levels of competition and he liked to construct new plays--all the time. He was a true student of the game.

He was also a very good health and physical education teacher and was always a cheerful sponsor of extra-curricular organizations. I always will remember one story he told me about one of his health classes. All the students were asked to fill out questionnaires. One of the boys answered the sex identification question with the answer "occasionally." Such a simple, silly thing became a comic rite when Murphy told it.

Murphy was also a good Space Cadet companion of social studies/political science teacher Billy Byerly. When those two got together to "chaperone" a student trip,, to intercede for a noble student cause, or simply to "outhustle" some of the other faculty members verbally in the halls, you had to watch out.

Byerly was nothing like Murphy except for his prankiness. Murphy was a clean-cut, jock-type. Byerly had been in the midst of the late 60s protest movement. The long, fuzzy-haired Byerly had a big, furry mustache which made him look exactly like "Today" show regular Gene Shalit. Byerly had also played in a folk-rock ensemble while a student at Oak College (I had not known him there) in North Carolina. His band, "The Great Atlantic and Pacific Jug Bank", was a big hit with the locals in Piedmont, North Carolina.

I got along well with Byerly, and with Murphy. I played and talked basketball with Murphy; I played and talked folk-rock with Byerly. In school, we all three played guitars, played basketball, and entertained students and fellow faculty alike.

Byerly was the resident radical at Winding. I was the resident reactionary (or, at least that's what Byerly called me; however, he called anyone a reactionary whose politics were a bit to the right of Ho Chi Minh). We often combined our classes--usually my U.S. History and his political science--to give the students two dramatically different views of contemporary history. Byerly was never so excited as during the Watergate investigation. He grinned like a crazed hyena.

Yet, with all of our apparent differences, we respected each other because we knew that each was trying to make students think. We dramatized the issues. We debated, we downright argued--in front of students. We performed. We were involved. We were good models, I would like to think. The students knew we were sincere about our subjects, about education, about them. It showed. We were not two young men who had decided at the last possible minutes in undergraduate school that we would choose teaching as an alternative to accounting, the law, or medicine. We were sure that we were teachers.

Even if Murphy and Byerly occasionally did weird things, they were a credit to the profession. One day, Principal Leonard was looking for Byerly and Murphy, near the end of school. It was about mid-day, the dogwoods and azaleas beautified the countryside, the air was sweet, and the strawberries were ripening in Tidewater Virginia. Leonard finally discovered that his two energetic teachers had gone strawberry picking since both had planning periods during the last period of the school day.

Winding High School was a relatively small school in eastern Virginia. It catered to an agricultural community. It was fortunate to have at least three Space Cadets, maybe four. Four? Yes. I think that I began to recognize some of the preliminary "symptoms" of Space Cadetism during my three years at Winding. Indeed, even more than my education courses in undergraduate school, the Winding stint put me in touch with my true feelings about teaching. I was beginning to "learn what I had done." But, at Winding, I was still an observer, still teaching what I was taught.

CHAPTER SEVEN
TEACHING WHAT I WAS TAUGHT (PART II)

"Listen, you, either clam up and take notes or I'll run you outta here" I barked at Lenny Barnes as he plagued the quiet girl next to him. "Remember," I said, "Clam up not shut up!" There is a degree of nicety about clam up. You get the message across without resorting totally to uncivilized techniques. Lenny knew what I meant, but there was one thing Lenny could not learn to do (and he wasn't alone). Lenny could not learn to love lectures every day the way I had absorbed them at Oak College. A steady diet of lectures had made Lenny lose whatever zeal he had for Nefertiti, Julius Casesar, Charlemagne, and Napoleon. Yet, by the end of my first semester at Winding, I still had not learned that one should not lecture every day. That was something that I had not learned in my "Methods and Materials of Teaching High School Social Studies" at Oak College. What could I do to improve the situation? If only I had asked that question as early as my junior year in college! Luckily, I did ask it before too much longer.

Periodic reactions by students during my first year of teaching never were seen as reactions to methodolgy. My response to anyone who suggested such would have been, "That can't be, what do the students know about methodology or curriculum development?"

In retrospect, I can't understand how I failed to observe Billy Byerly's methods. We even team taught. I noticed that Byerly did not always lecture. I just assumed that Byerly was doing simply one more thing to subvert society (this was pre-Teaching as a Subversive Activity). I wish now that Byerly had subverted my teaching techniques. He probably was doing that all along, subconsciously.

When I began my first year of teaching at Winding High in the fall of 1971, I began my career under less than favorable conditions. America was still ensnared in Viet Nam. Racial misunderstanding was at a peak. Urban violence had not subsided substantially and had even permeated the rural areas. Winding was a small town in the midst of an agricultural county. Yet, by 1971, Winding High School (with 50/50 black/white student ratio) had tasted the bitter

50

fruits of the turbulent 1960s. Everyone hoped that the 1970s would usher in a calming period. The calm had not come, nor were there signs of calm, by fall 1971.

I was twenty-one years old, a single male, a semi-jock, who knew just enough not to realize my shortcomings. I was really beginning my education rather than ending it (as I probably thought). I believed, rather simplistically, that I could go into class and spout off the lectures that I had cribbed from my Oak professors' notes (with a few gems from primary and secondary sources). In fact, that's exactly what I did the first traumatic year at Winding. The fact that I was young and inexperienced mattered less than the fact that I was virtually untrained in curriculum development. Age in teaching matters little if the teacher is mature enough to understand disparate personalities and is willing to be flexible. But beginning teachers are often resistant to change.

My insistence on coaching was both a plus and a minus. I had been a good high school athlete. My college experience amounted to trying out for the baseball and basketball teams and not staying with either. I lost interest in baseball. The basketball practice schedule became too rigorous. Coach Million, as I've said, was a slave-driver (even if he was a Space Cadet. Million must have had something to do with Pygmalion in the Classroom). So, I still had a burning desire to coach. Maybe it was to extend my youth. Maybe I perceived coaching as an avenue to adulthood and authority. At any rate, coaching was different from teaching. When we were in the gym or on the playing field, most of the players seemed to be in a better frame of mind. I'm sure the play element was a key factor in their better psychological state. I have thought about the play element in teaching for over ten years (I have not thought about it as much as the Dutch medievalist Johan Huizinga did--his Homo Ludens: A Study of the Play Element in Culture is a book that every teacher should read).

It was pretty obvious that players were students on the field or in the gym. They were in a learning environment. But, they seemed to be happier at learning in the play environment. What were the reasons?

Thus, Viet Nam, racial violence, and a desire to coach were three factors that influenced my first three years of teaching. There were many others.

That old cliche about teachers learning by teaching, I thought, was a bunch of baloney. Oh, it may be for some teachers, I thought, but not for me, not for me. I think that I thought that way because I had never taught before. To admit that teachers learn by teaching was to admit that I hadn't learned anything — because 1971 was my first year. So, having learned all there was to learn in undergraduate school, I set out to mesmerize about 180 students at Winding High. Some were turned off immediately. Some actually responded positively to my austere lecturing. The latter were the ones who would have learned if the teacher had been a deaf mute (of course I didn't realize that at the time).

As green as I was, I took the role of teacher seriously. I was Thomas Becket after he became Archbishop of Canterbury (I didn't realize that my teaching methods would be murdered). To me, I was in a proud and noble tradition. I was to impart the wisdom of the ages to a bright, fresh, new generation. And, I still believe that. Unfortunately, because of many forces beyond my control, I wasn't looked upon (nor were my colleagues) with the same esteem as I had looked upon some of my teachers in high school. Things had changed and I didn't like the changes. While I was trying to become the model teacher, I had become the Model T. In the late sixties, I had learned the lessons of teaching in the 1950s and 1960s (and, I'm sure from some teachers and professors, the lessons of the 1940s). Now the 1970s had blown in and changed the rules.

CHAPTER EIGHT
TOYING WITH TRANSFORMATION

Even while Winding High School was in the throes of racial integration, as was almost every school district south of the Mason-Dixon Line, I was experiencing a type of knowledge integration which would continue to shape my thinking about education in the decades to come. I was unaware of the change beginning to take place. In retrospect, I am hesitant to point to a specific factor which began the change. In this chapter, I will reflect on the beginning of a transformation in my whole approach to education and to life.

My first day of class was exhilarating. After a few minutes in homeroom--that wasn't so hard--I met my eleventh grade U.S. History students for the first time. Indeed, they were my first real students of all time. That was a problem that could have been alleviated. On the contrary, I learned while I earned.

I had had all the methods courses and the various psychology courses at Oak College but I had not student taught. Indeed, I had refused to partricipate in the student teaching routine. Against almost all well-meaning advice, I elected not to student teach. That hare-brained decision on my part could have been more disastrous than it became. I was at the tail-end of the teacher-shortage period in the early 1970s. Somehow I got a job.

One thing's for sure, my teaching style during those first two years at Winding was entirely not my own. I taught what I was taught. Most of the time, I cribbed my Oak professors' lectures and added a new wrinkle here and there.

I was so inebriated by my own rhetoric the first few days of class that I barely noticed that I was the only one listening. The students put up with my lectures the first couple of weeks--I was new, I was young, I was full of baloney! Unfortunately, those qualities bought only a few short weeks of academic serenity. The honeymoon was soon over. The grim reality of the next eight and a half months was soon staring us all in the kisser.

Jimmy Bradley was the first to crack under the excess strain of my lectures. Bradley was a nice, clean-cut blonde boy who also played football for me. But, even nice, clean-cut football players can wilt under the oppressive heat of too many lectures. One morning in mid-September, at about 9:10 a.m., with the morning sun illuminating the institutional green classroom, Jimmy stood up and yelled something obscene to an old man who happened to be passing outside our wing of the high school. The old man turned toward the classroom and looked quizzically, unable to determine from whom (or what!) the noise came. The class howled.

"What did you say, Jimmy?" I asked in alarm yet pretending not to hear the remark.

"I didn't say nothin'," was Jimmy's stoic reply. The class howled again.

"Are you trying to tell me that you didn't say anything, or yell anything?" I inquired further.

"Well, yes, I did say somethin', but it was only to break the monotony," Jimmy said honestly (although I was galled by the sarcasm of the remark).

"You get right down to the office, young man!" I ordered angrily.

"I'll be down in a few minutes!" I added.

After that incident, my U.S. History course got worse. Teaching, or what I thought was teaching, became an unbearable chore — except on days when everyone was listening. There was never a general revolt, but the next three months were extremely difficult because I was slow at getting the students' silent messages. They were communicating to me in various ways that I should mix up my pitches, throw a few curve balls, a few knucklers, a few changes of pace. They learned to hit my high, hard one in only two weeks.

If U.S. History class was bad, world history class (my favorite), was worse. True, there was the two-week honeymoon with the new teacher and the first of the year feeling out period. Why, I was so ill-prepared for the non-academic rigors of public school that I even smiled before Easter. And, even though I was too dumb to get student messages, the students were smart enough to get all of my signals — most of which I was too dumb to know that I was sending. One message was my poorly organized daily schedule, characterized by my smile. The students quickly learned that I was "Easy Rider." I gave assignment after assignment, day in and day out, believing to the letter some friend or relative's remark that lots of homework will cure the ills of education. So, I poured on the coal. Soon, I was so swamped with papers that I got little else done. Most of the assignments were of poor quality. I should have given about one quality assignment per week rather than five, six, or seven poor quality assignments. I would call a quality assignment any assignment, written or oral, that encourages the student to think about the subject in question and encourages him to analyze the facts and bring his own personal experiences, beliefs, and knowledge to bear in formulating an answer if a question has been asked. For example, if a student were studying the Constitution of the United States (which we did in the fall of 1971), he might be encouraged to read about the men who drafted the constitution and asked to put himself in their shoes. Or, the same student might be asked to compare the U.S. Constitution with other constitutions and asked to evaluate both (all) on the basis of "protecting human rights."

A poor quality assignment is one in which the student is asked to find answers to specific questions without being forced to think about both question and answer. On Bloom's taxonomy, the "knowledge" questions, if given all the time, would be poor quality questions. However, the knowledge questions, if used sparingly and effectively, constitute a vital part of the learning process.

Unfortunately for American Public Education, I learned in my first year that ineptitude was being practiced by ten and fifteen year veterans down the hall. My excuse was that I had not student taught and was in my first year of teaching. What were their reasons? Even heads of departments were teaching as they had been taught. Ninety-five percent of them were lecturing every day and giving poor quality assignments. Almost everyone. Billy Byerly and Rex Murphy were the exception to the rule. But aren't all Space Cadets exceptions to the rule?

Principal Leonard was impressing us with his Space Cadetism at this point. He was really pushing in-service training (as a good principal should!) He was particularly innovative in fostering behavioral objectives (oh, ghastly things!). I, and many of my colleagues, were not impressed. We all huddled together at lunch, in the teachers' lounge (that den of vipers) and after school to complain about behavioral objectives and other "bureaucratic boondoggles" which stand in the way of the teaching process. Even poor teachers ("those who teach even when they hate it") complain about "bureaucratic boondoggles" which obstruct good teaching. Many of the teachers I've seen wouldn't know good teaching if they saw it. Yet, even though I griped about Leonard and his ridiculous behavioral objectives, I secretly liked the idea of learning something new and keeping abreast of innovations in the field of education. Shouldn't all good teachers feel that way? Or, is keeping up with innovations in the field of education the solitary realm of Space Cadets?

In the fall of 1972, one year after beginning my teaching career, I decided it was time to go to graduate school. I was accepted by Old Dominion University in Norfolk and began working toward an M.A. in history. I signed up for two courses that fall. One, a diplomatic history course, was a killer. I was teaching four courses at Winding, coaching basketball and baseball, and was squiring Miss Reich around. Professor Woody at ODU took no mercy on me. He required a short paper every two weeks and oodles of book reviews. I spent my half-hour lunch, mornings before school, planning periods, and study halls preparing for that course. I talked with my world history students about diplomacy. At times, though the schedule was rigorous, I found my students and I were enjoying this course in diplomacy. Indeed, I believe that my graduate school experience made me a better teacher. It kept me in touch with history, with professors, with another level of the teaching profession. I was constantly learning.

My course in historiography was good primarily because the professor required us to read a great book, Gilbert Highet's The Art of Teaching. I have since read and re-read The Art of Teaching. It is always refreshing. It cuts straight to the heart of teaching. You can't be a real Space Cadet unless you read The Art of Teaching. You do want to be a Space Cadet, don't you?

"Winding High will accept almost anyone," was the caption under the yearbook photo of Mr. Leonard and what appeared to be a heinous-looking creature. The creature had a skeleton head and was garbed in a black cloak and hood. The photo of principal Leonard and the monster had been taken on Halloween (an appropriate enough time for monsters). The monster had been seen hulking through the halls of Winding High. He . . . er . . . It would appear almost magically outside the door of a math or English class. The first unsuspecting student to spy the monster did not know whether to laugh, run, or yell. Finally, other students would see the creature and, finally, the teacher at his desk would know something was amiss. Usually, the monster would vanish before the teacher realized what was happening. At the next door or at a door in another wing of the high school the monster would appear again.

"Who is that weirdo?" Coach Murphy asked Billy Byerly.

"Search me," Byerly said, "Must be some Space Cadet!" The weirdo was me.

Even during my first two years at Winding, I decided that school had to have its fun, off-the-wall moments. I decided that Halloween should be celebrated at school — during the school day.

Many of the students were stunned when they discovered that I was the man in the monster suit. Somehow, it didn't fit their teacher image. Teachers didn't do that sort of thing. Teachers were inhuman machines who made students' lives miserable for seven hours a day. Most students believed that teachers spent their evenings doing dull things like preparing ways to plague students. Even though many students decried the stereotypical behavior of teachers, they really were unable to accept an alternative to the stereotype. Long before I became a good teacher, I decided not to become like the stereotype.

I made a vow before I began teaching that I would uphold standards — standards of academic excellence as well as hygiene and image. Somehow, I found myself in the minority regarding dress.

The seventies had begun to loosen the hold of dress codes. The liberation ethic of the sixties had done its job. Ph.D.'s looked like survivors of Woodstock or Altamont. The attainment of an advanced degree was a signal, it seemed, to loosen one's personal standards. The advanced degree was taken by many to mean it was okay to be a slob. It didn't take long for public school teachers to take the hint. The seventies had people believing that clothes didn't make the man. No one knew what did make the man but almost everyone knew clothes didn't (Bill Blass, eat your heart out!). Yet, something coaxed me to dress fashionably — as fashionably as one can dress on a $6,700 a year salary. Students needed guidance in almost every phase of life — even in how to dress. I believed that professionals should dress like professionals.

Most of the Space Cadets I have observed in the teaching profession were knowledge integrators. They knew a lot about a lot of things and they always took time to explain how different subjects fit together. When I came to Winding High, I decided that I would show my Winding students a little bit of me and a little bit of the interesting and dashing things I had learned from the likes of Mrs. Shoe, Mr. Brucie, and Professor Ancient from Oak College (although I did not know at the time what I had learned from anybody). I was determined to give my charges more than I was given — which wasn't much, mind you. Aside from learning to read and do a bit of notation (not writing, notation), I learned very little in my twelve years of public school. It was a good thing for me that I went to college. I had to make up a lot of lost ground at old Oak College. And, I think I did! Yep! Give them more than I got. That was a type of educational capitalist work ethic. Didn't your middle income parents strive to give you more material things than they were given themselves? Well, I strive to give my students more of learning, life, and me than my public school teachers had given me.

But, as I've explained, I was ill-prepared for my 1970s students. Even though giving them what I learned in college was something stimulating, it was not nearly enough. Yet, I stumbled on. I genuinely cared about my students. I tried to talk to them on their levels - occasionally (although I thought and still think that teachers should encourage talk with students at the teacher's level - occasionally, assuming the teacher's level is higher than the students').

CHAPTER NINE
THE DISCARDED IMAGES

Ill-prepared wasn't the word. Sometimes my lectures were given to twenty-five zombies, not real people (or, most probably, they were not heard by twenty-five real people who did not want to listen to a would-be-teacher). Boredom begat trouble. Soon, about late October, I was beginning to have trouble with a handful of students. The ones with the long attention spans, the G.T.'s (gifted and talented, academically gifted, or whatever the current appellation happens to be), gave me no trouble. Anyone can teach the gifted. But I had more than the gifted — a whole lot more! How could I reach them all? This question is fundamental for all teachers: How do I deliver the message? Sure, the gifted and above average can soak up a lecture a day and never tire of it. But, what about a student like Darrell Tyrone?

Darrell was a worker, not a brain, but an intelligent boy who was continually badgered by his parents because they lauded praise on his younger sister, Maureen, for her straight A's. Darrell was a good sport, however. He never punched out his sister.

I empathized with Darrell. I kinda liked him. I was and still am a soft-touch for a hard worker. Darrell wanted to improve himself. He did. I talked with him about the sibling rivalry. I explained to him how he could make the B-honor roll. He was interested. He did it!

Giving special attention to individual needs is a mark of a Space Cadet. I believe that my understanding that every student had quite a different set of needs was a sure sign of the onset of Space Cadetism. I believe that my portrayal of the Halloween monster was another. Another was my performance with Mr. Byerly.

Byerly had grown up in Winding playing guitar and other stringed instruments. He had played in a couple of bands. So had I. When we met each other we talked about rock and folk music, the Beatles, and other pertinent topics. Billy was a folk-rock addict who could not outgrow his need for rock.

Both Billy and I believed that teachers should not be stereotyped, that they should enjoy life and be models of happy people. It has been my observation that most teachers are not happy people. Maybe it's the low pay. Maybe it's the low self-image. Maybe the low respect by the community. Maybe it's the little hell-raisers in the classroom. Whatever it is that makes teachers be bores and losers, Billy and I were determined to delete that trait from our vocabularies and the vocabularies of Winding students and parents. Billy, looking too much like Gene Shalit, and I, conservatively dressed and groomed, decided to play our music for the school.

Billy and I practiced for a few weekends, sometimes to the dismay of our wives. We worked on a few originals and, of course, ballad-types that two guitarists could play. Billy did a first-rate job of Ian Tyson's "Four Strong Winds" (that may be in my top ten all-timers), and a remarkably fine performance of Stephen Stills' "4 + 20." I sang "You've Got to Hide Your Love Away" by the Beatles and Gordon Lightfoot's "If You Could Read My Mind." We also did a few originals that I wrote.

The students loved us. They were shocked at first. Stunned looks turned to snickers. Snickers became good-natured respect. We were pretty good there in the Winding gymnasium. It was sort of like a Simon and Garfunkle with Garfunkle the dark-haired one.

The Point: The students saw us in a different light. We were, all of a sudden, much more than lecturers, chalk and pencil pushers, and grade givers. We were doers. We could still cut the mustard. Right then and there, we were transformed. Space Cadets must be able to cut the mustard. They're the teachers who can intrigue, who entertain, who go the extra mile, as it were. Billy could do that. In retrospect, I think that I was beginning to enter into a transformation. However, it was only the beginning. I still reverted to teaching what I was taught.

One day after school as I pushed the grocery cart through Nedd's Super Market, I turned the aisle of cereals to see one of my students, Mickey Devane, standing there beside his father, Mickey's mouth wide open. I thought before I spoke.

"Even teachers have to eat, pay bills, and fix the air conditioner,"

I explained to Mickey (all the while wondering why I was explaining).

"But . . . but . . ." Mickey stumbled. It was not yet fitting his neatly ordered universe. In his universe, teachers gave assignments, gave a lot of boring lectures, graded papers, and lived happily (or, boringly) ever after. Boys played football and baseball and sometimes gave teachers and parents a tough time. Girls wore dresses, smelled good, and were on earth to follow the wishes of boys. I really believe that seeing me in the supermarket was a great learning experience for Mickey. Oh, down deep, he probably thought that I was some fag in there pushing a cart and teaching that history. I also think that men teachers didn't fit Mickey's universe. The idea didn't really fit Mickey's father's universe either. Indeed, if I were a betting man, I'd say Mickey and his father were a pretty fair cross section of American children and parents whose idea of a teacher is a faded, wrinkled forty-eight year old woman in glasses and sporting a bun of hair and last decade's clothes.

Speaking of clothing (which I plan to do on a few occasions in this book), maybe clothes no longer make the man or woman, but I'd much rather see a well-dressed man or woman than the sloppy, out-of-style, lethargic-looking messes I've seen in classrooms across America. Maybe the sloppy dress of the late 60s and early 70s was a blatant reaction against Wall Streeters and General Motors' men who wore $400 Brooks Brothers' suits, $40 ties, $60 shirts, and $250 shoes. Teaching, a liberal profession (it has been called both a subversive and conserving force), was in a state of disarray in the 1970s. The Me Generation, pop culture, Viet Nam, the Civil Rights' Movement, the Woodstock Generation and other energetic, justifiable — albeit counter to the status quo — forces had America in a tizzy. The teaching profession felt the shock waves of those experimental years. Many self-styled teacher radicals intentionally wore un-corporation looking attire. Teachers wanted to look like students. Needless to say, standards were lowered. The dress codes of the 1950s and 1960s gave way to mini-skirts (Kinda liked them on my female students), longer hair and facial hair on males, longer hair on some women's legs, and other styles considered alternative (and sometimes downright decadent) to the status quo. I became something of a Space Cadet at Winding because I tried to dress as neatly as possible: two and three piece suits; slacks and woolen plaid jackets, and ties everyday. I was a professional and I made every effort to wring a pro look out of that $675 per month that I took home.

I believe that teachers who have lost their standards (or who never had any) are losers and part of the problem of American education. They are the blind (and ragged) leading the blind. In a way, it was fairly easy to be a Space Cadet at Winding. The competition wasn't that stiff. Yet, there was Mr. Leonard who dressed like he stepped out of Gentleman's Quarterly; there was Byerly, who could argue any conservative on any subject; and, there was Murphy, the creative coach who was at home in the company of English teachers. They were the three Space Cadets at Winding High School who gave the school its flavor and flair. By the end of my three years at Winding, I was beginning to discover that I thought very differently about education than a majority of my colleagues. I dressed differently, thought differently, and oftentimes (such as when I dressed up as a hideous monster) I acted differently. At the time, I knew I was changing my whole outlook. Yet, I didn't know exactly what you called someone like me. Maybe Murphy said it best, to Byerly one day in the hall after lunch:

"That guy Carter there . . . is a real Space Cadet."

CHAPTER TEN
THE FIRST PAINS OF TRANSFORMATION

As I mentioned earlier, I believe Space Cadets must integrate different fields of knowledge. They must bridge the gaps between diverse fields of inquiry. A Space Cadet who teaches science cannot cut himself off from physical education, math, and history teachers — and still be a great teacher. An experience that I had at Winding High helps to illustrate this point and I believe is the real beginning of my own intellectual and pedagogical transformation.

My first year of teaching brought about my intense desire to show students how English and history accentuate each other (and, maybe, how other fields of knowledge might be integrated with these two), that history teachers should strive to learn all they can about literature, and that literature teachers should learn all the history they can. A young man related to me, as I discussed transcendentalism in American thought, that he knew of another Ralph Waldo Emerson. Since he was in my American history class, he thought he knew something the teacher did not know. He had heard of another Emerson in literature class.

A few minutes later, the same young man realized that his Emerson and my Emerson had both composed essays entitled, coincidentally, "The American Scholar." Then, coincidence of coincidences, my young learner found out that MY Emerson had also published a famous essay called "The Conduct of Life." Finally, my student realized that HIS Emerson and MY Emerson were the same character. "Why do we talk about Emerson in history class and English class?" was his innocent inquiry. "Because history and literature are married," I tried to explain. "They are inseparable, just as Romeo and Juliet were inseparable," I added with a bit of schmaltz. "Each one gives life and illumination to the other — Emerson was a literary figure, but his writings played a significant role in history." From that first-year-teacher experience until now, and on junior high, middle level, high school, and college levels, I have made it my business to correlate language arts and social studies (English and history).

An historian (history teacher) in the public schools must not overlook the poems, plays, the music or the fads or historical periods. They also help to create or illuminate the overall picture of an historical epoch. An English (or other literature teacher) teacher cannot escape the ever-present realism of chronology and historical perspective in every literature unit. The marriage of Clio (the muse of history) and Shakespeare (as good a symbol for English and English literature as I can come up with at this time) can fulfill history and literature classes.

By correlating language arts and social studies, you are helping your students across a very difficult educational bridge. In our world of departmentalization and specialization, we sometimes forget that there are a great many of us who have to be taught that the King Hygelac (Beowulf's Geatish King) we read about in <u>Beowulf</u> in our literature class is the same one mentioned by the medieval chronicler Gregory of Tours <u>(History of the Franks)</u> which we heard about in history class. Literature teachers who take the time to teach historical background, as well as history teachers who take the time to incorporate literature into their classes, are helping students across the difficult educational bridge. As I've pointed out a number of times, knowledge integration is a primary trait of the Space Cadet.

This story is just a mildly painful part of an individual's personal transformation. Sometimes, the process is more painful.

There are many obstacles to integrating fields of knowledge. If you happen to teach in a junior high or high school, the curriculum design itself is a very obvious deterrent to knowledge integration. Our public school system is carefully planned to obstruct integration. And, if that isn't enough to do the trick, many teachers themselves may stand in the way of knowledge integration — and true education. An interesting situation I experienced at Winding High illustrates further what I'm saying.

Having been a history major in undergraduate school, I was put through a rigorous writing program. Frankly, that was a natural occurrence. Historians write, why not history majors? Therefore, I decided that I could do a lot of good for a lot of students by teaching the essentials of research paper writing in my history classes. I had probably written more in undergraduate school than most English teachers had.

But, try as I may, I had teachers who believed that history teachers should stick to teaching history — and leave the teaching of writing to the English teachers. I mean, hadn't English teachers always been the ones who taught writing? If so, they had not done as good a job as they would have liked to think. Something had to be done. I decided I was the one to do it.

I had written several term papers in undergraduate school. Professor Ancient had required one in each of the four classes I had taken with him. True, writing was a pain. Historical writing may have been a severe, head-splitting pain. I had breezed through my English writing asssignments. One had been on Julius Caesar (I was integrating in my sleep. It had me by the ball point pen!). I ended up my essay believing that Caesar had been a misunderstood fellow. Had I been introduced to Shaw's Caesar and Cleopatra sooner, I would have known that that conclusion had already been etched in marble. Another essay in English was my attempt to understand my motivation to marry. Professor Bland (no joke intended) had liked that one. In addition to writing historical material in English classes, I had already begun to make knowledge integration a part of my thinking even as a sophomore. Professor Ancient and a couple of others seemed to mix disciplines beautifully, like a good bartender can mix gin and tonic. Sure, Ancient was an historian, but he realized that a good teacher — yes, an S.C. (Space Cadet, if I haven't used that term enough already) — had to travel throughout the universe of learning. As I said earlier, I wanted to convey this idea to my students. To me, then, knowledge integration seemed at the ground and root of education (I seem to think that way still).

Yet, a storm was brewing at Winding High in 1972. Rhetorically, the idea of a history teacher "helping" an English teacher sounded quite plausible, even inviting, to the English Department. In fact, they hated it. They thought I was an alien, on alien turf (I didn't realize it then, but shouldn't Space Cadets be on alien turf?).

Nevertheless, I pushed on posthaste.

"Now students, today we are going to begin our research projects!" I beamed and was met with a multitude of facial expressions. Larry Barnes hated the idea that forced him out of his early 1970s lethargy. Petunia Petite loved the idea. She liked any thought-provoking idea which encouraged her to add to her storehouse of learning. I had a class of thirty-five and they all fell between Larry and Petunia.

What better way to accommodate all those diverse learning styles than to put each individual on a topic and allow him to work at it at his own pace (assuming, of course, that his own pace allows him to finish before the end of the millenium!).

"Okay, ladies and gentlemen," I bellowed, "You may choose one of the selected topics on the sheet (I said as I disseminated my suggested topics list), or you may develop your own topic."

Then we were off. We spent many days just thinking about our topics and writing about what we were going to write. Some days we stayed in the library browsing through the stacks and compiling a bibliography. The whole nine weeks were devoted to the project (which, theoretically, is still not enough time). I mean, there I was, in my second year and I was already showing definite Space Cadet signs. All of the signs were completely beyond me. All I was trying to do was get through the year, but at the same time, entertain, help students learn, and learn how to learn. The English department didn't see it my way. They squealed to Principal Leonard.

"Mr. Carter, would you stop by Mr. Leonard's office on your way out today," the secretary, Mrs. Bright, spoke matter-of-factly into the microphone. Almost all of my students loved it when Mr. Leonard asked a teacher to come by the office. The students seemed to like to see the teachers on the hot seat. Some even wished that certain teachers would be severely reprimanded.

"What's old Leo want with you, have you been gettin' outta line?" Larry Barnes asked sarcastically.

"Do you mean Mr. Leonard?" I asked Larry.

"Yeah!" Larry shot back.

"I suppose he just wants the opinion of his favorite teacher!" I said to a chorus of boos and hisses (good natured boos and hisses, of course).

The 3 p.m. bell rang. The students filed out eargerly.

"You may stay until five and drink your fill from the fountain of knowledge," I teased Misty Jones as she angled by my door.

"You may have my portion, Mr. Carter," she shot back. I was amazed at her ability to respond within the metaphoric context.

The hall became ghostly quiet as it did everyday at 3:10 p.m. I shut the door (yes, room 222, honest!) and began the trek — across the breezeway (I think principals always put Space Cadets as far away from their offices as possible) — to the main building to talk with that short, feisty, nervous man, Mr. G.L. Leonard, principal (remember, he always told students, "the last three letters in principal spell pal!"). I wondered what my pal wanted with me. The gestapo-like tactic of announcing to the whole school that you are to report to the principal is very unnerving, even for a veteran second year teacher. I truly empathized with students.

Mr. Leonard asked me into his office. Inside, I looked at the usual principal memorabilia: a framed certificate pronouncing Leonard a member of the Knights of the Blue Nose, an Air Force group; three diplomas, one from Florida State Christian College, wherever that is! He had two large framed prints of some big-eyed, big-headed children; I can't remember the name given to this artist's work. These, I suppose, were to put students at ease when they came to the office. Leonard also kept a rather extensive library for a principal. There were more there than the ever-present volume of School Law, a volume of Anecdotes for School Administrators, and other sundry tomes. On top of a book case were various sorts of figurines and sculpture.

"Sit down, Mr. Carter," he said calmly and hospitably.

"Thank you," I responded politely.

"Mr. Carter, are you trying to start a war with the English Department?" he asked trying to make light of the situation.

"What exactly do you mean, Mr. Leonard?" I asked unknowingly (although I knew fully well what was going on).

"To put it bluntly, Mrs. Crane came in today during her planning period to complain that you were attempting to do the English Department's job," he explained.

"Someone has to!" I shot back.

"Now hold on!" Leonard's fur was a bit fluffed at my rather unkind statement.

"Oh, I'm just kidding!" I said (I usually was just kidding, I think).

"What are you going to do about this unpleasant situation?" Leonard inquired.

"This so-called unpleasant situation just happens to be a very good learning experience for my students," I told Leonard more than he cared to know.

"I know!" he said quickly.

"I . . . ," before I could get the words out, I realized that he had agreed with me. I was ready for a long, hard battle. I knew that, then, Leonard was a Space Cadet, First Class, who happened to be principal. I also knew that as principal he had to keep peace among the faculty at Winding.

"Go ahead and teach the term paper," he instructed, "Just don't tell anyone!" he grinned and conveyed to me that he understood what I was trying to do, but he had to make Mrs. Crane, as the English Department head, feel as though she had some power.

Mr. Leonard's support of me reinforced my ideas about knowledge integration. I believed then and I still believe that a teacher's main task is to help students understand the goodness of the past and to see how each part fits in the whole mosaic of learning and life.

Somehow I didn't expect my colleagues at Winding to be obstacles in the way of knowledge integration. I thought they would be facilitators. Only a few were, specifically Leonard, Byerly, and Murphy. Community people and kids themselves I expected to be awed, infuriated, and reluctant when faced with the prospects of a new paradigm. I thought about the community as an obstacle when I made my first grocery shopping trip in the small community of Winding. I pushed the cart like a good grocery shopper should. I filled it with some of what I needed and much of what I didn't need. I turned a couple of corners and heard a familiar voice say, "Mr. Carter, what are you doing in here?" On several occasions during my first three years as teacher, coach, writing instructor, and other roles, I had asked myself the same question.

CHAPTER ELEVEN
RECHARGING BATTERIES AND TRANSFORMING

"I suppose I could collect my books and get on back to school . . . ," Rod Stewart lamented in his hit song "Maggie May." "Maggie May" is my second all-time favorite song (even though John and Paul didn't write it!), partially because it describes so accurately my state of affairs in early 1974. I was at a crisis point in my life, educationally and domestically. It's funny how one kind of transformation syncretizes with others. Synchronicity was happening. Part of my transformation was sad — for me anyway. It involved an attempt at marriage for all the wrong reasons (I'm still not sure what all the right reasons are). The attempt failed. But, my transformation as a teacher continued.

For two years, Miz Reich (that's what her students called her) and I struggled to develop a "social unit" (gee, what a stupid, meaningless phrase, like so much static sociology), to try and have a home, learn each other's moves (sorta like learning your tennis partner's moves) and be professional teachers. We failed.

We weren't too far apart educationally. We both believed that teachers should put themselves into their jobs, teach those suckers something and set good examples for them. That was all we had in common. So, as part of my personal transformation (I know the word "transformation" is in vogue these days, but like the word "feudalism," there is little descriptive substitute for it), we parted company. That chapter of my life, which had a few interesting paragraphs, was over. Neither of us looked back. That's good, methinks (I always liked the expression "methinks," makes me feel quite Chaucerian). Now, that we've had a bit of a personalized tragic interlude, I must confess a more contemporary problem which just occurred. That problem is this:

I just ran out of ink, right here in 1985. My expensive Paper Mate ball point, the black, thin kind with the medium point, has run dry (just like Eric Clapton's and Jack Bruce's seeds were going to do in Cream's song, "Sunshine of Your Love" — my black, thin Paper Mate loved words until its seeds ran dry). I was sitting at the pool, soakin' up them (Poetic License #16616910) rays, writing away, when drizzle, fud (and other sundry onomatopoeia), the Paper Mate ground to a halt. I wish I could write this book at the typewriter, but I can't. I know, Tom Robbins does that sort of thing. In Still Life with Woodpecker, he sprinkled his story with reflections on his typewriter. He wrote as though he were composing at the typewriter. Lucky fellow. But, I'll wager that even typewriter composers get the blues (except maybe for Erica Jong). Now, I've sat here for ten minutes wondering if I'll go get a pen back at the room here at the Atlanta Hyatt Regency, or if I'll just soak up rays and fall asleep. No, I am going to the room to get another pen. The show must go on.

I am back. Wasn't that fast? The maid helped me out a bit. She left her maid cart unattended. Nestled between the matches, French milled soap, bath gel, plastic bath caps, and clean towels was a stack of fresh black Hyatt Regency Hotel pens. They have the Hyatt logo on them — an impressionistic H which looks like a Rohrschach. There's one on the bottom of the pool, on the small pats of butter, and on the desserts at Hugo's, one of the Hyatt's restaurants. It's amazing how a Hyatt impressionistic H can increase the cost of a bowl of ice cream. Only a teacher would observe that! That keen power of observation has come from fifteen year of low salaries. If I were Kurt Vonnegut, I could say "And so it goes" at this point and have a rather nice, if shaky, transition back to my tale of transformation. But, I'm not and I don't have a rather nice, if shaky, substitute (like the Hyatt pens for the Paper Mate — I should get some help toward writing this book from the Hyatt people for that $80 a day room rate; however, I don't feel pressured by humanitarian concerns to acknowledge Hyatt or the maid in the preface).

You can tell that my relationship with Miz Reich was a strong one. She got one paragraph in this book and the Hyatt Regency Hotel in Atlanta and its black ball-point pens got a page. That's right, no looking back.

It was early 1974, U.S. involvement in Viet Nam was over. I was left wifeless. What to do? I tried to size up the situation. What was stable about my existence? I thought I was a good teacher trying to get better. I had decided long ago to try my hand at graduate school. I was in Virginia with no strings attached. I had already applied to two or three graduate school. My new girlfriend, Gretchen, had already decided to go back to UNC-Greensboro to graduate school. Why not? I was accepted by their grad school and given a graduate assistantship. I got my books and went on back to school.

In both a scholarly and utilitarian way, the year at UNC-G working on an M.A. in history helped. The three years at Winding had sapped my energies. I really needed to recharge my batteries, learn some new material, and sit at the feet of a master. I remembered that Professor Ancient at Oak College had suggested UNC-G for medieval history if I wanted to stay in the area. Professor Baker, the medievalist at UNC-G, was a scholar of international renown. So, it was off to UNC-G, to be with Professor Baker and Gretchen, who came along at just the right time. Rather than obstruct my basic transformation tendencies, as Miz Reich had done, she facilitated transformation.

Graduate school at UNC-G was anything but a snap for me. Maybe it was for others, but not for this boy. Professor Baker was determined to turn me into a medievalist. Reading courses with him were grueling. I had to devour everything and then have my brain picked. Research papers and seminars added to the work which was really a difficult delight. I worked hard and my efforts paid off. In the summer of 1975, I received my M.A. degree and was awarded the Draper-Gullander-Largent Graduate Prize in history, the department's annual award to those individuals showing scholarly promise. What UNC-G did was to make me believe I had some ability. Boy, is that ever the coveted characteristic of a good teacher--make people believe in themselves. Professor Baker, as tough, austere, and ornery as he was, believed in me and believed that I could go on for a Ph.D. In fact, at that time, I don't even think that I believed I could attain a Ph.D. I'd just gotten an M.A. and, in August, 1975, a wife--Gretchen (who also obtained an M.A., her degree was in speech pathology). What we needed were jobs, not more graduate school.

In addition to the extensive subject matter I attained at UNC-G, I gained further benefits. Remembering the trouble I'd had with the

English Department at Winding High, I was determined to become an English major. I began that task at UNC-G, taking a couple of English courses that would help me attain a North Carolina teaching certificate in English. I had to practice what I preached about knowledge integration.

I also learned important teaching techniques at UNC-G. The methods course I had had at Oak had not prepared me for teaching history/social studies in the public schools. I had always learned much more from observing Space Cadets and their strategies. Even in 1975, I remembered clearly the methods and mannerisms of Mrs. Shoe, Mr. Brucie, Professor Ancient and the few other Space Cadets that I had observed in my quest to be a teacher. I learned a great deal more from Professor Baker: how to write clear, succinct lectures; how to deal with students one on one; and, most of all, I learned more than I ever had about the writing process--from a history professor, imagine that!

Teachers in public schools I attended had talked a good game about the importance of writing, but none of them (not even the Space Cadets) had done anything about it. Indeed, if I had any criticism of my Space Cadet teachers in the public schools, it would be their lack of writing for journals and newspapers. Some of them could have done it, too. I believe, in fact, that Mr. Brucie went on to receive a Ph.D. in Middle Eastern Studies after he left our high school. So, I know he wrote a dissertation and, in so doing, was forced to go through the writing process.

Baker put me in tune with all of the journals and big names in medieval history. He really wanted me to pursue my interest in medieval history. I have loved the Middle Ages since I read "The Golden Apples," a tale about a poor boy who became a knight and had to ride up a glass mountain to get three golden apples, and since I watched El Cid (a.k.a. Charlton Heston) ride off along the Spanish shore. I cried. I mean El Cid was the "Old Yeller" for future medievalists of my generation. I guess all the budding American historians cried at "Old Yeller" and "The Alamo."

In educational circles, the belief is that there are two kinds of good teachers, the Librarian, who works prodigiously, austerely, modestly; and, the Cowboy, the rambunctious, vain, effective, motivator of men and women. Baker was a Librarian. Ancient had been a combination Cowboy/Librarian. In fact, by 1975, I had never observed a real Cowboy teacher.

Having Baker as a model, I became convinced that writing was the important part of one's education. I had written relatively little before I met Baker, although I had written research papers and essays and a little poetry at Oak College. But Baker was a scholar, and, in the firearm, Victorian Lamp, and book-filled office at his home, he was continuously cranking out book reviews, articles for Speculum, the medieval journal published by the Medieval Academy of America, and books. I learned first hand what the writing process was all about. The biggest writing lesson came while I researched and wrote my M.A. thesis under Professor Baker.

Because I was attempting to complete the work for my M.A. in a year, I had to research the thesis from the time I enrolled at UNC-G. Baker put me through the paces. I was writing about his subject, Anglo-Norman history, so he knew all of the primary and secondary sources.

My reading courses with Baker gave me ample opportunity to take copious notes on secondary sources that I would need for the thesis. Long sessions in Baker's office also allowed me time to pick his brain about the feasibility of my topic long before I had suggested the topic to him as a potential thesis. When it was time to suggest a thesis topic, Baker was sure that I was a serious student. I had good study and work habits and I read voraciously. When I suggested my topic to Baker, he consented right away.

Baker read every chapter word for word, letter by letter. He made copious notes in the margins and had me rewrite every sentence that was not up to his standards. He was the sternest taskmaster I had ever faced. After I had completed the first draft and I thought I was home free, Baker annihilated my manuscript with an artillery attack of red marks. But, I was going through the writing process. The process is never easy. It is always demanding. It can turn your hair grey. By the time I finished I had almost as many greys as Phil Donohue (my mother said they made me look distinguished to which I related my dislike for looking distinguished at age twenty-five). When I wasn't working in the UNC-G library, I was working at Gretchen's apartment on Tight Street (Haight-Asbury writ small in the late 1960s and 1970s, with a touch of Beach Music and Soul). Unfortunately, when I worked outside the college library, I had a pen in one hand and a Viceroy in the other. Hard, scholarly work seemed to beg for a cigarette. The jock of 1966-67 has become the smoke-stack of 1974-1975.

My brain and psyche were being transformed and my lungs were being coated with poisonous, life-killing fumes. Yet, I was only twenty-five and the entrophy was not yet apparent. I smoked a pack and a half of Viceroys--no, it was probably two packs by August, 1975--a day and still had the wind to play an occasional one on one or two on two basketball game. I didn't feel a thing, or did I? The morning cough, the morning cigarette, the phlegm were all tale-tell signs that, friends and neighbors, cigarette smoking was like slow suicide (I know Kurt Vonnegut has already written that, too. He said that his brother was committing suicide by cigarette). I spat, gagged, choked, basketballed, and wrote my way through my M.A. thesis. Smoking was definitely not helping my personal transformation. But, no time to worry about that then. I had to get a job. Gretchen had to get a job. Since we were recently married. we both decided that jobs in the same part of the world would be feasible (don't laugh, we, and probably you too, have friends, husbands and wives, who work in different cities or different states). It is a sad commentary on our times that husbands and wives who want to be professionals must suffer the pains of social mobility and flux. Unfortunately, that is a fact of modern professional life. If you want to be a Space Cadet, you must direct your space ship to the right planet. There are planets (school systems) that would love to have an alien Space Cadet come and infuse new life into their sagging educational structures. If your domestic life will allow it or, if like mine, it forces you to do it, go and try your hand at teaching in a new place. I did and it helped rejuvenate me.

It was only three weeks until the deadline for submitting theses for binding that Dr. Baker alerted me to the fact that he demanded a first rate thesis--get this, even if I had to come back for an extra semester. I was terrified. My life (and Gretchen's) depended on our getting jobs. Indeed, we both had already acquired jobs in Cumberland County (Fayetteville is the largest city, you remember Hay Street?). I had been offered a job (which I accepted) by Fayetteville Academy, a private school. Gretchen had been offered a job by the Cumberland County Schools.

The Fayetteville Academy people had hired me because I had coaching experience. The advertisement in the Greensboro Daily News had announced a vacancy for a basketball coach and a social studies teacher. My three years at Winding had given me the necessary experience. I wanted to integrate sport and physical education with academic disciplines.

Little did I know that the Academy people liked my shiny new M.A. How many North Carolina private schools boasted a basketball coach with an M.A. in an academic subject? I mean, that's no great shakes, but I know for a fact that I was the only M.A. in history at the helm of a private school basketball team in North Carolina in 1975-1976. I was cool, I suppose.

The year and a half between January 1974 and August 1975 had been a major part of my transformation. It was even visible to me then. The three years at Winding had been my teaching maiden voyage. I had tried to put everything I could into my first three years. In fact, I sometimes put too much of the wrong thing--too much lecturing (although a good teacher would never be afraid to lecture on his subject--what Gilbert Highet wrote in The Art of Teaching in 1950 is just as applicable today), too much inconsistency (this is one of the most important things a good teacher does, maintain consistency).

Although the 1974-75 period, vital for my transformation, presented to me a visible road to transformation, I did not know at the time what I wanted to be transformed into, what transformation was, or whether one could even be an active force in one's own transformation. By 1974, I had not yet read Thomas Kuhn's The Structure of Scientific Revolutions, one of the ground-breaking books for the idea of tranformation. I suppose I was like most public school teachers, practicing what I thought was my craft, taking graduate courses in education or in a subject field (I took history at UNC-G), and generally being led away from many of the powerful books that had been written between 1945 and 1975. No one ever mentioned Kuhn's book. Oh, some teachers and principals were reading Alvin Toffler's Future Shock in the early 1970s, a few were even into some Americanized forms of Buddhism; yet, no one ever brought the name of the book The Ultimate Athlete by George Leonard into the lounge in 1974. The physical education teachers I knew, even Murphy, were totally oblivious to the "big books" in their field. They were more interested in strategy books by Dean Smith or Don Shula and in their female students. Many coaches I have known have espoused the philosophy that high school girls are fair game for their amorous desires. The ribald movie satires of the late 1970s and early 1980s such as "The Last American Virgin" "The Cheerleaders", and other soft-porn pictures, are truly not that farfetched. When I was a teacher at Winding High, my fifth period study hall was often interrupted by a student from a certain physical education teacher's room. The note always asked the same question: "Mr. Carter, may I see Linda _____ in my office during this period?" Never dreaming what was going on, I blindly sent Linda over to Mr. _____'s class. I would never have known anything except that one day, I used my fifth period study hall as an opportunity to go and see Mr. _____ myself--about a matter far removed from Linda. My trip to his office, near the gym, was quite innocent and unpremeditated. I had thought about getting Mr. _____'s opinion on a fund-raising project for the school that I had planned. True to form, right at the beginning of fifth period, the student arrived from Mr._____'s office. The note was the same. Off Linda went.

About fifteen minutes later, I asked my colleague next door to keep an eye on my class (good teachers never leave their classes unattended). He said he would (he'd better say "yes" after all the times I've watched his hellions during the past three years).

I arrived at Mr. _____'s office and noticed the office door slightly open. No one was inside. The door to Mr. _____'s shower room was shut, I noticed as I glanced quickly around the barren office (barren except for a collage of basketball players that one of Mr. _____'s female players had created for him).

I ambled into the office. I took it upon myself to see just what kind of shower room Mr. _____ had. I opened the door quickly. I heard what I thought was a body hitting a shower curtain. Naively, I said, "It's Mr. Carter." Mr. _____'s voice pentrated the quiet. "Carter, what are you doing here?"

Still not seeing the panties, bra, and dress hanging on the shower rod, I answered, "I wanted to see what you thought about a student-faculty game to raise money for the school.

"Sounds great!" he said.

I saw the undergarments. Needless to say, the pieces of the puzzle flew together. I decided I should ease out of the shower room and forget about this embarrassing situation.

I never mentioned the incident to anyone. I tried to forget it. But every time I saw Linda in the hall, she always smiled that smile. If she did when I called the roll, I never knew. I never looked back there. I guess that's what stunned me. That sixteen year old girl could carry on an illicit affair with a thirty-five year old coach in the shower room at school and be cool as a (not cucumber, too common) Trane Air Conditioning salesman. I suppose I wasn't cool. More people seemed to be reading Marcuse than Kuhn, more Hefner than Niebuhr.

CHAPTER TWELVE
ONE MORE TIME ... COACHING

In 1980, Marilyn Ferguson wrote The Aquarian Conspiracy: Personal and Social Transformation in the 1980s. She, in synthesizing much of the new wave, whole earth knowledge of the 1960s and 1970s, explained that as a person experiences the first pains of transformation, there is a period of ambivalency. The old ways of thinking and doing are hard to shake. They are at war with the new ways of thinking and doing. Reading this book in 1982 helped me to understand what I was in 1975-76 (if only we could synchronize the books and the time! Who will tell me what I was in 1984, maybe some former used car salesman in 1990, or some former Professor of Sociology in 1992; maybe a new Leo Buscaglia or Norman Vincent Peale or Gail Sheehy in 1995; maybe some new Adalberon of Laon?). Adalberon, the bishop of Laon, wrote a poem, "Carmen ad Rothbertum regem" in ca. 1025 in which he drew up his famous tripartite division of medieval society: "those who fight," "those who pray," and "those who work." Ole Adalberon helped whole generations understand themselves and their place in society in his poem (or at least his poem helped twentieth century medievalists form an idea of how medieval writers saw their own society). Maybe another Adalberon will do that for us in ca. 2000 or ca. 2020; he'd, or she'd better hurry though. I've promised not to read any more poems after 2065--I'll be 116 then.

At any rate, Ole Marilyn Ferguson showed up about seven years after 1975 to write that book which helped me understand how I was in 1975. I clung to the old ways of thinking all the while developing new ways of thinking. I could even see this war being waged (Zoroastrian style) in myself then but I didn't, couldn't understand it. I only began to understand it in 1982 when I read Marilyn's book.

One particular illustration underscores my hesitancy to make the transformational leap from learner to teacher in 1975-1976. Indeed, it may have been 1976 when I made the break from the past (not a complete, historical break--a true transformation is never a complete break from the historical past; it is a situation in which the past melts into the present and the future (T.S. Eliot said it so much better in "The Wasteland"). It is nearly a Toynbean transformation, such as when the declining Roman world melted into the newly emerging Christian Middle Ages. A new being was created, a Christian Roman World that had elements of both the old and the new. On a microcosmic (maybe microscopic is the right word) scale, I was a miniature world transformation (holographical, isn't it?) in 1975-76. I clung to the past and my old ways of thinking and at the same time embraced certain new ways of living.

I have been involved in and with sports since before I went to elementary school. Boys' Club sports in elementary school came first. I was a junior high and senior high quarterback in football, guard in basketball, and pitcher/first baseman/third baseman in baseball. In college, I even played a bit of basketball as a freshman. At Winding High, I had coached basketball, football, and baseball for three years. The old had a hold on me. I was not yet ready to make the transition from jock to knowledge integrator (because, for one thing, I probably perceived, incorrectly, that the transformation required that I give up athletics). I took the job at Fayetteville Academy. It went like this.

"Show me a good loser and I'll show you a LOSER," snapped Vince Lombardi, the near-lengendary mentor of the two-time Super Bowl Champion Green Bay Packers. GOOD GUYS FINISH LAST blared the title of the book by the aggressive and sometimes comic player and coach Leo Durocher.

"Winning is not the most important thing in life; it is the only thing," reiterated Lombardi and repeated by numerous college, high school, and arm-chair tacticians in America. The last time I heard words like those was at my high school's awards banquet at the end of my senior year. The football coach from Famous University was asked to speak to us on subjects similar to those about which Lombardi, Durocher, et al have raved.

I was caught up in the spirit of being an American, teenage jock, of being a relatively successful high school quarterback, guard in basketball, and pitcher-infielder in baseball. I made all-conference in basketball and baseball my senior year. College athletics became a reality.

Somewhere between September of 1967 (the date I entered college) and January of 1971 (the date I completed my B.A. in history) something happened to me. In the fall of 1971, I found myself the coach of a high school junior varsity football team. I thought I still wanted to play. Yet, I found that the teaching of history mattered more to me than the 'busting' of heads on the football field. We went two and four and I knew something was wrong--two wins and four losses for a fellow who had once played on a state championship basketball team which had gone undefeated in twenty-six games. Had I atrophied that much?

I completed my M.A. in history in 1975, and, lo and behold, secured a job as social studies teacher at a private school in the eastern part of North Carolina. The position also demanded that the teacher be the head basketball coach, though not necesarily in that order. That's right. I became the head basketball coach at that private school--the school reportedly placed a high premium on learning. I was thankful. I thought of myself as a well-rounded, Renaissance Man.

My plan was to create the well-rounded basketball player, the scholar-athlete--look out Cecil Rhodes! There were a few athletes around who did not seem to fit the typical jock mold. I was determined to mold more. I wanted a thinking team, win or lose!

"Win or lose, win or lose!" repeated Mr. Boyt. "You will win a few games for us, won't you, Coach Carter," the board member asked frantically as he smashed his umpteenth Camel unfiltered into the UNC Tarheels-emblazoned ashtray?

"Sure, we'll win a few and maybe even lose a few." I assured him, although I could tell by the strained face that Mr. Boyt believed his beloved sport...er... school might be in trouble. However, I had them over an academic barrel. They needed my M.A. degree-they were gearing up for an accreditation by the Southern Association of Secondary Schools and Colleges. Thank God for master's degrees and headmasters of private schools or whomever or whatever it is that demands brains as well as baskets--I was in.

My players wanted to be flogged every practice. They wanted to be tortured upon the medieval rack that is called "a good practice session."

We were three and five at Christmas. I was frustrated. I knew my approach of understanding and good teaching was sound. Unfortunately, not too many others agreed with my philosophy. They also seemed to have grown up with that "to win is human, to lose asinine" philosophy. I couldn't believe it. Old ladies were literally throwing things at referees. And the language! Lenny Bruce would've been embarrassed to sit in the gym on some nights.

I am not a drill sergeant. I am Thomas Aquinas on the basketball court. The players resented losing like a kitty resents having its stomach fur rubbed the wrong way. My constant reminder to be good sportsmen became more and more a symbol of weakness to the players that I was trying to reach.

The end of the long season finally came. It really happened! As luck would have it, and to make matters worse, we made it to the tournament, the last place seeded team out of a field of eight teams. I continued my "onslaught" of reminding my team to be thinking men and good sportsmen. By the time of the first round of the tournament, they were almost snickering at the team prayer, an institution reflecting some culture in athletics.

To add insult to injury, the girls' basketball team was knocking off one opponent right after another. Inevitably the bus rides back from many games carried two types of creatures: the cheerful, confident female and the sulking, irritable, insecure male. At the end of the regular season the girls' team and their Vince Lombardi-mold coach had a record of fifteen wins and three losses. My team's tally was twelve wins and eleven losses. I was keeping my word to the private school board member--win a few, lose a few. To a fellow who was born and bred on winning, a twelve-eleven record was the end of the world.

We played the second seeded team the first night of the

tournament. We somehow killed them psychologically because they had to go home and tell that they were beaten by us, 47-45. When I went to school the next morning, I met the athletic director going through the front door. He had helped me through the gloomy months of December, January, and February. However, he expected to hear a familiar result. I had to help him keep from falling when I told him the score of the night before. We both agreed that miracles do happen in the twentieth century. Two nights later we had an easier time of it, disposing of the fifth-seeded team, 59-43. Miracles come in bunches, I've been told. "Are you kidding, they're not really in the finals, are they?" an unbelieving "supporter" of ours inquired. "I'm afraid so" laughed another confident fan.

Everyone knew the coach and team would return to being Cinderfella and a pumpkin this night. This night was the night we faced the regular season champs, a team that had beaten us both times during the regular season.

They began beating us their methodical way in the first half. We were down by 11 at halftime. We threw in the towel and had another prayer before taking the court in the second half. I pounded once more the good sportsmen routine. I figured this would be my last chance to get it across to these particular boys.

All appeared lost. That is, if you consider winning the conference championship the most important thing in life. As for me, I felt that we had already won a lot. We had beaten two teams no one thought we were capable of defeating. No one had gotten hurt. And, I had just received my federal income tax refund. I could already envision my players refusing to shake hands with the victors at game's end. I still don't know why but they did not have to refuse my command to be good sportsmen. They won--or was it, I won? I'm still debating that question, too.

We went ahead for the first time, 43-42, with ten seconds to go in the game. Even then I could not accept the fact that we were near to winning the conference tournament championship. Then the real miracle happened. A veteran team with a veteran coach--a team and a coach that were confident of winning--failed to get off a shot in ten seconds. I, I mean we, had won the conference championship in my first year as head coach of a varsity team.

After we received our championship trophy I won my first real battle in life. My team was awarded the best sportsmanship trophy for the season. Lord, was I proud.

I decided to retire after that season, at the ripe old age of twenty-seven. My wife Gretchen, who had struggled through the depressing year with me, agreed wholeheartedly with this decision. I still teach because I believe teaching is a way of introducing young people to the great ideas of Plato, Aristophanes, Augustine, Boethius, et al. I retired undefeated at one win and no losses. One championship and one good sportsmanship award, the best award young people, or any age group, can win.

I used two shop-worn sports cliches at the athletic banquet that year--after that championship season. One was a rather naive, as almost all athletic sayings are, mixed-metaphor I borrowed from golf: "It's not how you drive (meaning our poor season start), it's how you arrive (you guessed it, the conference championship)." Then I turned to an old saying that my father repeated to me often as I was growing up. It is a statement that I believe will never lose its meaning or flavor. We have come to a point in our history when we tend to turn our collective noses up at the alleged old-fashioned, down-home remedies for sick bodies and sick souls. I told those people in the banquet hall that I had lived by and would always live by what Grantland Rice wrote:

> *When that one Great*
> *Scorer*
> *Comes to write*
> *against your*
> *name,*
> *He writes not that*
> *you won or*
> *lost*
> *But how you played the game.*

Winning may be the most important thing in life, but it is not the only thing. Losing is a part of life, too. Losing makes winning more meaningful. It makes it sweeter. It demands that we savor those precious moments.

Life is not all smooth-sailing and rose gardens. It is not all winning. Constant winning is no challenge to the winner. Winning, losing, winning, losing follows the general pattern of life closer than constant winning, or constant losing for that matter.

The fellow who can win, lose, take it in stride, pick himself up by the bootstraps, and dare to win again is the real winner. When your young athletes come home after school or after a game, ask them if they won or lost--sure--but also ask them how they played the game.

CHAPTER THIRTEEN
TOWARDS TRANSFORMATION

Although I had taught for three years before going to graduate school at UNC-G, I really date my major transformation period to the years 1976, 1977 and 1978. The three years I taught at Winding, full, taxing years, and the year I spent at Fayetteville Academy were still part of the learning process. I'm not saying that I did not learn after 1976. I am suggesting that my transformation, which began way back in 1971-72, did not flower until I burst through the cocoon of "teaching what I was taught." In addition to fighting out of that malaise, I had to become a concerned techer, a man who knew that teaching was his life-long calling. I began to know that after 1976. I'm kinda glad that it took place during the Bicentennial Year--what a red, white and blue experience--knowing who and what you are! Frankly, gang, I was aware that something was happening even in 1976.

The need to go to graduate school gnawed at me continually. My semester at ODU had only netted an historigraphy course and a course in diplomacy. Both, coupled with teaching five courses a day at Winding and coaching three sports, had worn me out. I decided in 1972 that if I had to get an M.A. part time, I wouldn't get one. The M.A. at UNC-G was tough for me but going full time had allowed me to get it. A year at Fayetteville Academy had made me realize that I should go back and get a Ph.D.--or try to get one. I applied to Duke University and was accepted. I had always been a closet Blue Devil.

But, just as Gretchen and I had made up our minds to move to the Durham campus, we decided that a Duke Ph.D. was too expensive. We opted out. I was totally frustrated (transformations are full of frustration). No job and no Ph.D. We went back to Fayetteville with our heads hung low.

Gretchen got her old job back in the Cumberland County Schools. My old job was taken. I went to the Cumberland County School Office--known affectionately as the White House. There, I talked with assistant superintendent Jamie Hawk. Hawk seemed to like me and told me to go see Principal Wally Capezio at Winner Junior

High School.

Principal Capezio immediately struck me as as an interesting character. He was an Indian who thought he was a cowboy. Everyday, we learned, he wore a suit with a cowboy string tie, a large cowboy belt buckle, and cowboy boots. This tall, slim, wavy-haired man quoted "The Love Song of J. Alfred Prufrock" by T.S. Elliot to me and I knew we were communicating. He hired me.

The Cumberland County Schools became the site for my transformation. I was a seventh grade language arts and social studies teacher when I got my first article published in 1976. My first article, a sure sign of my transformation, grew out of my graduate school experience at UNC-G. I was transforming. I could almost feel it, I could sense the growing commitment to education, to teaching, to learning, to life. I believe it was then that I was at the Frostian "road less traveled by." I suppose that I shall be saying all of this "stuff" ages and ages hence.

I performed well for Principal Capezio at Winner Jr. High. The language arts/social studies department asked me to be their chairperson. This, to me, was a great honor and another sign that something was in the air. When I realized that the school was undergoing accreditation by the Southern Association of Secondary Schools and Colleges, I was still honored. The accreditation proved to be a blessing. It brought me into contact with Clint Lipps and Desmond Fox, two consultants from the State Department of Public Instruction in Raleigh. Both of these men qualified for "Space Cadet" status on the first ballot. Both had been good teachers and now were good administrators and still good teachers. In addition, they both seemed to see potential in me.

Clint Lipps introduced himself to me when he came to Winner to observe our language arts/social studies department during the visitation week. Our school was being evaluated by the Southern Association and, if we passed (every school always passed), we would be added to the list of accredited schools maintained by the state and would be appealing to parents who lived in the Winner district. I'm glad Lipps was on the team which visited us. Not only was he a friendly and encouraging sort, but he was amenable to unorthodox methods and activities. His two colleagues, principals from other schools in the state, would have given us a poor rating for what transpired during the evaluation. Being a transforming teacher almost always means that your students will reflect some of your perceived eccentricities. Mine did, even in 1977.

My students and I had prepared dutifully for the evaluation team. The school was abuzz. Principal Capezio and his cafeteria manager, Mrs. Jukes, had feted the visiting team the night before with a rather elaborate dinner (elaborate when you compare it to the usual school cafeteria bill of fare--dieter's delight such as serving pizza, french fries, and sweet potatoes in the same meal; no wonder so many children go to sleep after lunch or hate most school lunches. Strange, the health and fitness craze which has swept the nation in the 1970s and 1980s has affected the public schools only minimally. Physical education is not mandatory for twelve years; kids aren't encouraged to eat nutritiously--that's part of the transformation also). A colorful, up-beat slide show had been produced. Old Capezio had outdone himself--this only added to my belief that Capezio was a Space Cadet disguised as a cowboy principal.

The visiting team was visibly encouraged and impressed. Only the live and in-color, in-class visits would be the tale-telling the next day. I looked forward to the next day's visit anxiously. I had prepared well, but you never know.

My activity demonstrated that classroom lessons are improved if the students had a hand in the planning and implementation. I mean, it's their education. Why shouldn't they have a say in it? We had been working on a unit (God, I hate that word--what is a unit? I know, don't define a Carnegie Unit, it is still senseless) on the Bible as literature. I always liked my "unit" (just like feudalism, there is no workable substitute) on the Bible because it infuriated everyone in the 1970s. First, the fundamentalists were alarmed because I even dared to mention the Bible in the first place (I thought that's what they wanted?). Second, the "new wave" coolies of the 1970s (parents who were part of the great un-churched, turned-on generation) were incensed that an English teacher was using valuable classroom time to teach religion. Finally, Capezio was concerned that an English teacher was getting so much flack. Even a Space Cadet principal has to be concerned about P.R.

"John," he said in his calm, friendly manner.

"John, I got a bit of a bone to pick with you," he said.

"What's the problem?" I asked amusingly.

"Mrs. Demeanor of the Parent-Teacher Council has reported that some parents are concerned about your interpretation of the Bible," he explained.

"How do they know how I interpret the Bible," I asked and immediately began to show irritation at the public's misunderstanding of methods.

"Well, you are teaching a Bible Unit, aren't you," he asked.

"Yes," I said shortly.

"How are you interpreting the Bible?" he inquired.

"I'm not," he answered.

"What do you mean?" he asked

"I mean that I am viewing the Bible as a piece of literature, like Shakespeare, Eliot, or Hemingway," I explained. I threw in Eliot because he liked Eliot as much as I did.

"I can understand that," he said, "but have you made that clear to the parents of the kids in your class?"

"No, I really haven't," I confided.

"You might do that," he said and I knew that he knew that I would straighten out the problem.

I solved the problem but our performance for the visiting team almost put me back on thin ice. As part of our study of the Bible as Literature, the students had been assigned the task of reading certain Bible stories and recreating them in a modern setting. Each of the four groups of students would present its "modernized" version of a Biblical story for the visiting team. Noah, Jonah, and Joseph proved to be very well interpreted, but the fourth and final version, "Sodom and Gomorrah," was a bell-ringer.

Four of the six students in this group were females. They went to the restroom to change into their costumes at the end of another group's presentation. The girls outdid themselves for authenticity. They marched back into the class in harem girl outfits--where they got them, I'll never know. Principal Lemon's eyes shone wide when the four girls strolled into room 222. The narrator told the tale and the girls began to bump and grind the modernized version of Sodom and Gomorrah. Just as the final grind was made, Clint Lipps rushed to the rescue.

"Mr. Carter, what we have seen today is an outstanding display of creativity on the part of the teacher and the pupils--we commend you."

Principal Lemon, a rotund lady in her early sixties, turned to her colleague, Principal Smith, another bespectacled, plumpish pedagogue. After what I thought was an agonizingly long time, Principal Lemon beamed and then lauded praises similar to those of Lipps. We had won.

Winner Junior High got flying colors from all the evaluators. Capezio was well pleased. The Space Cadets, it seemed, had scored a gigantic victory.

Clint Lipps really was pleased with my class. He used the opportunity of a post-evaluation reception to ask me to come to a summer writing institute at Mars Hill College. I would be one of twenty-five teachers of writing who would stay a week in the mountain hideaway studying the writing process and authoring a textbook on writing. I graciously accepted.

In retrospect, I find my invitation to this institute somewhat coincidental because I had just recently begun to exert a great deal of energy to writing and attempting to publish my writings. I was beginning to believe that I had learned something as a student and teacher and could find an audience out there in Reading Land. Indeed, 1976 and 1977 were banner writing years for me. Not that I had a great many pubications but I got cranked up. I began to believe that I was a writer and had something to say. I wrote. That was part of my self transformation. I went from thinking about writing to being a writer.

My first professional writings were reconstructed term papers that I had composed in college and graduate school and some poems. Strangely enough, my first submission was accepted by the Journal of the North Carolina Council for the Social Studies--even though I got a bag full of rejections after that. Yet, getting an early acceptance really acted as a catalyst. That was a giant carrot (as big as the one I saw on an advertisement in the Baltimore/Washington International Airport).

Writing became more and more a part of my teaching. Even while the National Council for Teachers of English was flexing its muscles to encourage teachers to put more emphasis on writing, I was doing it myself. It was a natural outgrowth of my own writing. I even found Donald Murray's A Writer Teaches Writing that year--and put it to good use. That book had been published in 1968 but I had never been introduced to it--principals were too busy with behavioral objectives.

As soon as school was out in June of 1977, Gretchen and I headed for Mars Hill. Gretchen was going to spend the week with our friends, Chuck and Elsie Wexler, in Hickory. I would then travel on to Mars Hill, about twenty miles north of Asheville, North Carolina.

I think the week was a stunning success and was vital for my transformation as a teacher. For one thing, I was able to devote an entire week to the study of writing. For another thing, I met twenty-four teachers of writing who might well have gone on to become Space Cadets. One in particular, Ellen Johnston, was a bona fide, card-carrying Space Cadet. Yet, of all the transformation activities and people I met at Mars Hill in 1977, two stand out: Desmond Fox and Reginal B. Schackman.

Fox was the director of the Division of Languages, State

Department of Public Instruction. He was Schackman's doctoral student. Schackman, who had been professor of English education at Duke University for nearly fifteen years, may rank as one of the most innovative Space Cadets of all time. It was Schackman, more than anyone else, who proved to me that it was okay to be a Space Cadet, that people really liked Space Cadets, that Space Cadets were great teachers.

Those two, along with Donald Murray and two or three other "leaders" at the institute, provided the guidelines for the week. We were instructed from 9 a.m. - 12 noon everyday. Every other workday minute was devoted to composing writing activities that would fill the proposed book of writing activities. I must have written at least a dozen different activities. The finished products were to be included in a volume that would be published by the State Department of Pubic Instruction. After some bit of humorous controversy, the title for the volume became "Writing in the Wild Young Spring." My suggestion was "Writings from Jupiter and Mars." Jupiter is just a stone's throw from Mars Hill. My title wasn't chosen. I thought it a bit spacey myself.

Among the many highlights of the institute, my trout-fishing expedition with fellow-teacher Jim Shuckberg stands out. An avid trouter, I decided that I could not pass up an opportunity to go trout fishing. Shuckberg, who had been taught by the Space Cadet Captian Schackman at Duke, expressed a lifelong interest in fishing. He also said that he had the required licenses, North Carolina fishing license and a trout stamp.

Unfortunately for Shuckberg, he was wearing the uniform of a 1960s radical, long hair and beard. True, he had a state fishing license and what appeared to be some kind of special stamp (I really believe he thought it was a trout stamp), the game warden could not go for the long hair and beard.

We had driven Shuckberg's car and were plowing around the banks of a creek that was a tributary of the French Broad River (Thomas Wolfe's stompin' grounds). We had both kidded about the "trout stream of consciousness" style of writing as we drove the ten miles to Weaverville (home of the Weaverville Milling Company, a very, very good restaurant--I particularly liked the steak terriyaki and the rum-laced strawberry-topped cheesecake). The fellow in the tackle shop in Mars Hill had directed us to Weaverville. He assured us that the streams had been stocked only a few days before.

Shuckberg took off upstream at what appeared to be a "fishy" looking stream. I went downstream and stopped under a nicely-constructed footbridge. I looked to my right upstream and saw Shuckberg easing his way through the stingweeds and Mountain Laurel. He finally flicked a salmon egg baited hook into the dingy water. I had had a night crawler in the water for a few minutes before and I worked it back and forth from the upper side of the big hole of water under the bridge to the lower side. I immediately began to think of onion sandwiches (which I hate). I almost always think of Hemingway's onion sandwiches (and flapjacks smeared with apple butter) when I'm fishing. I suppose I should think only of the flapjacks, but it's usually the onion sandwiches. "Big Two-Hearted River, Parts I and II" had a tremendous impact on me.

Just as I thought of the onion sandwiches, I heard a strange voice from atop the bridge above:

"Catchin' any?" the voice asked.

"Naw, I haven't even got a bite yet," I said without looking up, thinking that the voice must belong to the owner of the house on the other side of the stream and the fellow who must have built the nice bridge.

A few seconds went by. I looked back at Shuckberg, who must have been about thirty yards away, and noticed a khaki-colored game warden heading right for him like "Jaws" coming. They both walked up a partial path to the main road. I reeled in and began making my way through the stingweeds, thinking that something was awfully wrong for the game warden to take Shuck up to the road. Why, he had the required licenses. My hook hung in the weeds. I stopped and, when the hook did not fly free on my first tug, yanked hard and proceeded with a large catch of stingweeds. What would the warden want with old Shuckberg?

By the time I reached the two beside of the warden's khaki-colored car, he was reading Shuckberg his rights. He would not even listen when I tried to tell him that I would be stranded if Shuckberg had to follow him to an Asheville magistrate. Bye, Shuck!

Oh, they let Shuck out after a few hours. The game warden took him to an Asheville magistrate who only wanted $26.50 because Shuck did not have a trout stamp. What he had was a Pitt County fishing license. Shuck really didn't mean any harm. He just didn't have the right license, he just wanted to go fishing like all writers should.

While Shuckberg was being third-degreed by the Asheville magistrate (probably for having long hair and a beard), I was stranded in the trout steam. So, I decided to fish. I hoped that Shuckberg had called Desmond Fox or Reginal B. Schackman, or someone and let them know that I was braving June heat, rattlers, and loneliness while he was meeting Asheville's finest.

About five in the afternoon, Shuck came poking along in his sixty-nine Buick, looking carefully down at the stream for signs of life. When I saw him round a curve, I reeled in quickly and bounded up the hill, waders, stingweeds, and all.

What a story we had to tell the gang. It was the life of the late night story-telling sessions. But, for a few hours, I wasn't laughing at all. Transformation has scary parts.

I suppose every life experience can produce a piece of writing. Old Shuck composed a quite brilliant activity for students based on our trout expedition. Many good pieces of writing went into the production of Writing in the Wild Young Spring. Of my ten or so, the editors chose three. I was very appreciative. I went back to Hickory (and then Cumberland County) with renewed vigor.

Being with the 1977 writing institute was a major part of my transformation as a knowledge integrator. I had wanted to combine various disciplines since my undergraduate days. I had intensified my integration at Winding (remember the term paper that caused the stir with the English Department?). Then, there I was at the North Carolina State Department of Public Instruction with twenty-five English majors. Even though I taught language arts/social studies at Winner Junior High, I was still basically a history major who had transformed himself into an English and writing teacher.

I began to take courses in English and the teaching of the gifted and talented in Cumberland County. I had taken a few English courses at UNC-G while pursing the M.A. in history. I believed that a medieval historian could not do much without a knowledge of medieval literature. What good was the acquisition of fact after fact of Anglo-Saxon history without the flavor of "Beowulf," "Judith," or "The Song of the Rood"? Soon I had accumulated enough credits in English to qualify for N.C. certification. In addition, I decided to pursue the gifted and talented certification offered through the UNC-Chapel Hill extension program. I thought that I might as well learn something while I'm in Cumberland County. All the while, I longed for a chance to pursue a Ph.D. An Ed.D. would not do. All of my heroes were the Ph.D.'s of history. Somehow, someday, I knew I had to chase that particular Grail. I wanted to be the Frederic William Maitland from Leaksville, North Carolina, the F.W. Maitland that Professor Ancient talked about in those hushed, reverent tones. Yeah, I wanted to be like that.

And you know, I think that that "wanting to be" quality is a must for a Space Cadet. It means that you are alive and kicking (how many people still remember the group "Alive and Kicking's" "Tighter and Tighter"--if you do not, I'll excuse you as long as you remember the Easybeat's "Friday on My Mind"). "Wanting to be" a principal or assistant principal or a ballet dancer or a rock star or a professor of medieval history at Exeter is healthy. Every teacher should aspire to more than what he/she now is. Of course, the true Space Cadet will size up his present situation and decide what he has to do in order to be the best--now. If he is underemployed (which I was for three years), he still will make the best of it. I think the true Space Cadet believes what he is doing is the most important profession in the world. He believes that he is teaching the younger generation ways to think, to be human, to face the future. The true Space Cadet can hold his head up high as he converses with the local banker, the mayor, or a visiting dignitary from Washington or London. He must believe in himself even in the face of ridicule and distrust from his colleagues. He knows that he has crossed the Rubicon of professions. His fellow college graduates in business, accounting, and computer techology are talking to him about accounts, Wall Street, and six figures by their tenth high school anniversary. He must grit his teeth and respond with the facts that he is helping the next generation shed its cocoon and sprout beautiful magnificent wings--all the while bringing $1,000 per month and paying $800 for a house that is nowhere near the house that his lawyer friend got at a steal. I knew that Gilbert Highet talked provocatively about poverty among teachers when he wrote in 1950, but did he talk that provocatively? Did Gilbert Highet really have to sweat out a high mortgage and the heartbreak of psoriasis because he did not have the money to look like a preppie professor? We all want to be somebody. That's good! That's positive! Why settle for who we are? Space Cadets must continue to venture out into the universe of their minds in search of galaxies they never thought attainable.

Principal Wally Capezio, for example, wants to be a cowboy. He really is an Indian. He does have a percentage of Indian blood cruising through his veins. But, he's not satisfied being principal of Winner Junior High in Cumberland County (although he certainly is to be commended for his outstanding leadership which turned a rough and tumble school into a very successful one). In fact, I believe Capezio's encounters with cowboys accentuate his teaching and principaling. He understands fairness, the kind of fairness of the wagon train, the type of fairness John Wayne would be proud of. Whenever he encounters a problem at school, he not only brings his UNC-Chapel Hill Master of Education degree to bear on the situation, he is the trail boss who must decide. He is Gil Favor of the old "Rawhide" series. I think that I would like being judged by such a man should I be involved in an illegality at Winner Junior High School. The teaching profession definitely needs more Space Cadets in the principal ranks.

Meeting Fox, Schackman, Capezio, and a handful of other Space Cadets or semi-Cadets made 1976-1977 a banner year for transformation. Frankly, I still did not understand the whole idea of transformation at the time but I knew that I was becoming something more than I ever thought I would become. I was moving towards total transformation with lightning speed--or, so I thought.

CHAPTER FOURTEEN
IT'S A BIRD, IT'S A PLANE, IT'S SUPERVISOR!!!!!

Ever since Frankie West spouted off the line, "It's a bird, it's a plane, it's supervisor!," about Supervisor Byron of the Leaksville Schools, I've been saving it for the title of a chapter. I knew that it would one day be the title of a chapter about education, or students, or basketball. Mr. Byron followed us right up to the 3A State Championship in 1966. We played in Durham High School. The team stayed at the Jack Tar Hotel in downtown Durham. We were 23-0 going into the quarterfinals. A blowout over Roanoke Rapids got us a date with local favorite Durham Jordan High. We fixed D.J.'s clock with an impressive 84-66 win. Then, the finals. Our squad was pitted against Raeford High School and their giant center Mullin Moorefield, 6'8" of jumping energy. Somehow we prevailed over Moorefield and his colleagues and won for ourselves and our school a state championship. In the afterglow of victory, Mr. Byron the Supervisor walked into Shoney's restaurant and was greeted with the words which are the title of this chapter.

I remembered those words when I was appointed supervisor of language arts and social studies teachers for the Cumberland County Schools. I remember the day well. I happened to be jogging around Winner Junior High School the day the call came from Assistant Superintendent Hawk. Principal Capezio had turned a deaf ear and a blind eye to my jogging during my seventh (last) period, planning period.

Jogging had not yet become an obsession. Why, in 1976 I could barely make a mile and a half. I stopped smoking in July of 1976 amidst the usual gasps and coughs which come from smoking two packs of Viceroys a day. I felt terrible about telling Fayetteville Academy students not to smoke and then puff my lungs out in the privacy of my office. I couldn't live a lie or a fraud. I had to quit. I did.

Quitting smoking unleashed new energy. It was the engergy I needed to break on through to the other side of Space Cadetism. Before 1976, I had sapped my energy with nicotine. After I stopped the nicotine habit in July 1976, I found new reservoirs of energy.

My teaching improved. My writing improved. I could taste and feel again. Flowers reached out and touched me. I was alive with ideas and energy necessary to push them to fruition. My intellectual transformation was helped considerably by lungs that felt the cool crispness of fresh air for the first time in six years.

The new energy forced me into a new rhythm. I had lagged behind the natural earth rhythms from 1969 to 1976. But now, in 1976, I once again felt what I had felt as a child, as a teenager. In retrospect, I knew what George Leonard was talking about in his book The Ultimate Athlete when he described the primeval feelings attained from jogging. Jogging became the ultimate athletic, the ultimate cure, the time for preliminary planning. I took it in stages. First, a mile. Then, a mile and a half. Tom Roleski, a fellow English teacher at Winner High and I jogged everyday at seventh period, planning period. Tom was ahead of me, however. When I gasped for air in the blazing Fayetteville sun after one and a half miles, Tom would persevere on for another couple of miles. Finally, I pushed myself to the three-mile limit. It was about at that point that Assistant Superintendent Hawk appointed me supervisor of language arts and social studies. That was in the late fall of 1977.

My first supervisory job entailed part teacher and part supervisor. I taught two classes at Winner and spent the remainder of the day at the White House (administrative office) on Interstate 95.

I tried to improve the teaching of language arts and social studies as supervisor. I created a journal, Social Studies Communique with which to disseminate pertinent information about language arts and social studies to teachers in those subject areas. I really tried to make the LA/SS teacher feel important, needed, professional.

Whenever I visited a school, I made it a point to model new ideas and activities for the teacher. I spent the majority of my time in teachers' classrooms.

However, I found time to make presentations to state-wide meetings. In 1977, I watched almost spellbound as renowned educational author Bob Samples (no relationship to Junior Samples) delivered the keynote speech to the annual English Teachers Conferrence in Greensboro, North Carolina. In 1978, I delivered an address, and, I think, made a splash with some solid, creative ideas for teachers and writing.

My theme at the English Teachers Conference was "Turn on the Footlights" and it, I hope, encouraged teachers to stimulate students to write — lots and lots of writing. The belief was that if teachers expected students to write then the teachers themselves should set good examples. Having grown to adulthood in a period in American History which saw the demise of heroes (George Washington, we learned, wore wooden false teeth? We learned that Jefferson had black mistresses. Did real heroes make out with mistresses? We learned that Richard the Lionheart was gay). I was asking teachers to be heroic in an age when Dustin Hoffmans were replacing John Waynes! Indeed, one strong belief that has remained with me over the years has been my belief in the basic professionalism of the teacher. I have always thought that teachers should act professionally (even though being professional sometimes means "letting your hair down"). There is really only one major difference between a public school teacher with an M.Ed. degree and a practicing attorney: about $50,000 difference in annual earnings. I realize that this is the Olympian-sized straw that has broken more than one camel's back, but it does not have to de-professionalize the teaching profession. I harp again on appearance.

How can one be professional and not look professional? How can one expect a classroom full of impressionable students to be more than slobs if the only image they see for seven hours a day for 200 days a year is one of a slob? The money factor again plays a role. True, most public school teachers cannot buy Ralph Lauren suits or Saks dresses but most can dress professionally.

A male teacher can find bargains on clothes when department stores have sales. Charge cards have helped to allow people to wear now, pay later. I know that's not "pay as you go," but it's all most of us know.

Every male teacher should invest in some basic professional

clothing, even if it means sacrificing in other areas, such as entertainment. A man who would teach ought to own at least one basic three-piece suit. A teacher is always meeting the public: teacher conferences, visits with the superintendent, school open house, funerals, weddings, etc. If a teacher buys a basic navy blue threepiecer, preferably of a blend of 55% polyester and 45% wool (don't buy 100% polyester; students and parents who are fashion conscious hate 100% polyester; on the other hand, don't buy 100% wool, either, because it limits the number of days you can wear the suit), he can look professional and, whether the three-piecer is a navy or not, a navy blazer is a must. One is never out of time in a navy blazer — the Roman toga of today! One looks smart in a navy blazer. One looks ready to recite Shakespeare in a navy blazer. Then, after the three-piecer and the navy blazer, a male teacher should buy a winter-weight sports jacket, herringbone or tweed, and a spring-weight sports jacket, poplin, silk, or a blend. The sports jacket can be worn with many combinations of trousers: a black and white herringbone jacket can be worn equally well with the navy suit pants (but not too often with the navy suit pants or they will begin to look older than the navy suit coat), khaki pants, black pants, charcoal grey, grey flannels, and a few other colors — at least six good combinations. So, even on a minimal clothing budget, the male teacher can look professional. Many school systems have 180 days in their work year. So, if one wears the three-piecers sparingly, maybe three times a year, repeats the winter jacket cycle about four times (with six pants), repeats a similar spring cycle four times, he has covered one-third of the year. But that leaves two-thirds to go!

To look professional, one does not always have to be bedecked in a three-piecer, or even in a sports jacket. In addition to the above-mentioned gear, however, the male teacher needs to invest in a lightweight jacket (I think the thin Izod golf jackets are appropriate, or the still popular "Members Only" jackets, or the ever-present "London Fogs"). On many days, these can be substituted for sports jackets. Worn with a pair of slacks, a dress shirt and tie, they can make the teacher look well-dressed, sporty, dashing.

Ties are life-savers. They can help one do magic with a wardrobe.

The black and white herringbone can look forever young if the owner continually creates the fashion illusion of wearing more clothes than he actually has. A paisley one day, a military stripe the next, alternate the herringbone with the "Members Only," then a club tie with the herringbone, and colleagues and students will begin to call you Mr. G.Q. (Gentleman's Quarterly). Frankly, part of my Space Cadet reputation rests on my extensive wardrobe. Few of the other male teachers I have had for colleagues dressed as professionally. Indeed, many of them thought that I "dressed up" for school because I was on "another planet." I loved it!

I suppose it's part of the double sex standard in our society, but women teachers can get by with dressing professionally better than men. Many men teachers feel that they are expressing their masculinity by looking like slobs (don't get me wrong, a lot of female teachers have decided that they can express their masculinity by dressing like slobs as well). A majority of the women teachers who have been my colleagues over the past twelve years have dressed professionally. How do professional-looking female teachers dress?

No, it's not a $300 suit everyday (however, like I said for the male, having one good one doesn't hurt) but it's investing some money (and time) into looking professional. Women teachers have suffered the rap that they look, act, and dress . . . like teachers. The stereotype is the female English teacher who wears her hair knotted back into a "bun," wire-rims, and rather obviously old and out-of-date clothes. (There is a dilemma here: Should we, as teachers, forget about fads and fashion and show their basic ephemerality to students and dress like boobs ourselves?). Hell no! Let's take our stand as professionals! There is something rather unprofessional about a thirty-ish woman wearing 1960-ish bell-bottoms in front of teenagers in the mid-1980s. Don't you agree? Unless, of course, a teacher's basic space cadetisms allow her (or him) to make use of odd hair styles or out-of-date clothing. I know of some teachers who have used their archaic expressions and antiquated fashion to charm their students right out of the trees.

But, you ask, what's a female teacher to wear? That is the

question, for teachers and supervisors alike. First, there's nothing wrong with pants (provided, of course, they're on a man — just kidding). In the wintertime or during workdays (when books have to be lugged around and other chores are completed), what is more appropriate than pants on a female teacher? I mean, how would I like it if, during every move I made in front of thirty kids, I had to worry about exposing my underwear? I wouldn't like it. So, the conclusion is, female teachers should wear pants and attractive blouses and pant suits (not polyester ones, though) to school. But, dresses and skirts and blouses should be alternated as much as possible. A woman teacher, in a fresh cotton dress, hair nicely coiffeured, in decent makeup, is a professinal in every sense of the word (provided of course, she can teach).

Again, women should stick to basic clothing: a tan dress, maybe a stripe, possibly a plaid; a navy blazer, a business suit (see, even the suits are named for professionals in other fields. Why not a teacher suit?).

In addition to cheerleading for language arts and social studies I campaigned for better-looking teachers as supervisor — a space cadet supervisor. My boss, Assistant Superintendent Hawk, encouraged me every step of the way. I was being reinforced at every turn that being a space cadet was the way. I was teaching and learning right and left. I was coming to grips with myself. I was also on fire with writing. I was beginning to believe that I had the "write" stuff. As part of my push to improve writing, I was writing like mad. In the spring of 1978, my most successful book of poetry to date, Wampus Cats and Dan River Rimes, was published by Moore Publishing Company in Durham, North Carolina. The book chronicled my growing up in Leaksville, North Carolina and my reaction to the consolidation of Leaksville, Spray, and Draper into Eden in 1967. The book sold well regionally. I appeared on numerous morning talk shows in April, May, and June (particularly the "Good Morning Show," hosted by Lee Kinard on Channel 2 in Greensboro, North Carolina). All of a sudden, I realized that I was on a type of precipice. I could either continue doing what I was doing (It's a Bird, It's a Plane, It's Supervisor), or I could seek out a new type of learning. To everyone's surprise, I chose the latter.

CHAPTER FIFTEEN
ANOTHER KIND OF LEARNING

"Maybe you'd better take a few days off and go to Illinois and see what it's like," Assistant Superintendent Hawk suggested in an almost brotherly fashion.

"Are you sure?" I asked trying to divine his motive.

"Well, if you're going to do something as drastic as quit your job, you should be sure it's what you want," Hawk advised.

He was right. Being accepted for a doctoral program by an internationally-known university was inebriating. But, did it pay the bills? Would it ever pay the bills? Hawk was older and wiser and he seemed to really care about my well being. I had tried to give him and the school system 110% during the months that I had been supervisor. I think Hawk was merely telling me that he appreciated my work by encouraging me to test all of the angles before hanging up my supervisor's mantle.

Gretchen and I worried about the decision. Our parents had never had to make such decisions. Strangely enough, few of our friends, relatives, or even acquaintances were any help. Most of their responses centered around the idea: To give up two good jobs like you've got, pull up stakes, and move to a state 1,000 miles away to quest after a Ph.D. would take a man from outer space.

"We've got to do it!" I pleaded messianically. Gretchen knew I had to do it. She had heard it from her intuition. Going to Champaign, Illinois to "test the waters" was merely going through the motions. It was time for me to move into the next phase of my transformation as a teacher.

We assumed rather negatively that Illinois would be unfriendly and cold. We were right about the latter, however. Nevertheless, there were friendly and unfriendly types in Illinois as in all places we've visited. Of particular importance to our social well being was the fact that Reginal B. Schackman was now an English professor there. Schackman had moved there from Duke University a year before. He had encouraged me — at the Mars Hill writing institute — to consider Illinois for graduate school. I did! Schackman was a constant source of inspiration for Gretchen and me. I have never seen a more energetic or prolific writer. In addition, Schackman was a gourmet chef of the highest order. On several occasions during our two and a half year stay in Illinois, Schackman, Space Cadet First Class, treated us to chicken in aspic, homemade summer soups, salad dressings, desserts, and fine wines. We reciprocated as often as possible.

Professor Baker at UNC-Greensboro had believed in me so much that he wrote strong letters of recommendation for me to the handful of universities where I applied for doctoral programs. Illinois, among others, decided to give me a shot! I was determined not to blow my chance. I figured that a Space Cadet with a Ph.D. would be even more effective.

The grueling pace of the course work took its toll on Gretchen and me. The usual petty departmental politics made life interesting at times, bitter at others. Yet, I kept my sights on the goal, a Ph.D. in history (even though I had gotten certified in English and G.T., my first love was history).

Gretchen helped put me through the paces by taking a job in the Champaign, Illinois schools. Since she was a speech pathology major, the Champaign people grabbed her up. Coupled with my paltry teaching assistant salary, we managed to get by. Yet, all in all, it was a very exciting and enriching experience (for the most part).

My committee, Professors X, Y, Z, and O were a varied group of men. My dissertation advisor was a demanding individual who put me through my paces (as Baker had done). And, as if writing a dissertation wasn't enough, a catastrophe occurred.

"Look at him; just look at the scoundrel. And he is going to get away with it!" were the enlivened words of Professor Helen Maud Cam as she translated a detailed rape case from the London Eyre of 1321. Professor Cam, a leading scholar of medieval legal history until her death, responded quite humanely to a detailed fourteenth century rape case involving Joan Seler, the eleven year old daught[er] of Eustace the Saddler, and the accused rapist, Reymund de Limoge[s]. The appellee (the appellee in thirteenth and fourteenth century leg[al] terminology was the accused: from appellare, the Latin verb meanir[g] "to accuse." The word did not indicate moving a case to a high[er] court for retrial), a certain Reymund de Limoges, had been foun[d] not guilty by the London jury of 1321 despite the facts that t[he] appellant, Joan, had "survived the ordeal" of the fourteenth centur[y] English legal system. Professor Cam's spirited response serves [to] demonstrate the impact of rape even over nearly six hundred yea[rs] — the sympathy for a rape victim is not lessened by the larg[e] chronological gap.

As I studied carefully the proceedings of the case of "Sel[er] versus Limoges," a case heard in the London Eyre Court of 1321[,] I believed that I had found the proto-type of all thirteenth an[d] fourteenth century rape cases. This case was the most graphicall[y] detailed of all the ones I had studied up to that time. It was [a] veritable mine of information about rape, attitudes toward wome[n,] medieval sexuality, and the development of the English legal syste[m] in the thirteenth and fourteenth centuries.

The case involved the appeal of Joan Seler, daughter of Eustac[e] Seler, a craftsman of the London vintry of St. Martin's. Joan, ag[e] eleven, and her father appealed (accused) Reymund de Limoges, [a] foreign businessman living in London, of the rape of Joan's virginity[.] Joan and her father had followed the law specifically and had, firs[t] of all, given the hue and cry, the actual cry of rape after the attack[.] Then, Joan had reported the crime to respectable men of her village[,] then to the coroners at the Tower of London, and to a sheriff. I[n] June of 1321, she was once again repeating her story, this time t[o] the king's justices who were holding one of the infrequent roya[l] courts. The judicial scribes wrote in graphic detail:

> . . . He (Reymund de Limoges) . . . took this same Joa[n] the daughter of Eustace who is here, between his two arm[s] and against her consent and will laid her on the groun[d] with her belly upward and her back on the ground, an[d]

with his right hand raised the clothes of the same Joan up to her navel . . .

The sexual attack continued in the same kind of detail.

The phone rang. As I sat mesmerized by the case in the medieval room of the graduate library in a major midwestern university, I was disturbed by two, three, and finally four rings before the graduate-student library assistant answered the phone. I was deep into my doctoral dissertation. Jody's voice startled me as I sat with my back to the door. "It's for you, John," she said. "Okay, thanks," I replied. I put a paper at my reading place, closed the book, and walked the ten or twelve paces to the librarian's desk outside the medieval room.

"Hello," I said nondescriptly. "Johnny, I've got some terrible news," Gretchen's voice was almost ghostly. "Oh, no," I responded, "go ahead and unload it."

My wife did not let my insensitivity phase her. Her news was too horrifying.

"Cheryl's dead," she said bluntly.

"What?" I said loudly and then looked up to notice four or five readers turn their attention to me. I collected myself.

"Cheryl?" I asked.

"Cheryl the student-teacher I told you about," was Gretchen's only reply.

"That psychopath raped and butchered her," she explained in chilling yet placid remarks. She was obviously in shock.

"Oh God, no!" was all I could get out of my mouth.

Finally, I managed, "Where are you?"

"At the police station," she said.

"I'll be right there," I said without remembering that I had no transportation at the university. We both hung up without saying another word.

Without stopping to mull over what I had just learned, I interrupted James Pearl, a fellow graduate student and explained the awful situation. He immediately stopped his research, got his coat, and we hurriedly walked out of the graduate history library into the hallway. We nearly bounced down the three flights of stairs and into the bright sunlight of a cool St. Patrick's Day, 1980. James' car was parked beside a meter only a few blocks from the library.

We didn't talk on the way to the police station. The five-minute drive gave me time to think. The awful irony of the situation struck me. It could have been Gretchen. Thank God, it wasn't. My mind wandered back to the fourteenth century rape case involving Joan Seler.

By "surviving the ordeal of the fourteenth century legal system," it is implied that rape victims had to undergo procedures both inhuman and embarrassing in order to obtain justice. Even then, after victims had exposed their bloodied genitals to "reputable men and women of the village," to the shire reeve, to the coroners and, finally, to the king's justices (itinerant justices — proto-circuit judges), the chance for justice was undeniably slim. Why?

The office of coroner was at a rather primitive stage of development in the thirteenth and fourteenth centuries. As Dr. R.F. Hunnisett (of the Public Record Office in London, England) made clear in his well-known book The Medieval Coroner (Cambridge, 1961), the thirteenth and fourteenth century coroner was no modern TV Quincy. Investigative and gynecological techniques were unsophisticated, to say the least.

A second reason for a rape victim's inability to obtain justice was the body of distorted views about women which partially comprised the world-view of thirteenth and fourteenth century judges. The late English legal scholar C.A.F. Meekings, a former deputy record keeper of the Public Records in London, explained that thirteenth and fourteenth century English judges, though literate, capable, and possibly well-meaning, were, after all, people of their own time. They inherited the traditional views of women espoused by the ancient Greeks and Romans and by the early Church Fathers such as St. Augustine. Aristotle, for one, believed that women were basically inferior to men because he believed the "female semen" was less important for procreation than the male counterpart. The Roman Jewish scholar Philo saw women as aggressive beings seeking domination over men. Added to this dim view of women were the beliefs of the Christian church. In a remarkable article entitled "Medieval Medical and Scientific Views of Women" (Viator, 1974), Vern Bullough demonstrated how the Greek and Roman views of women were assimilated with the views of the early Church Fathers. Women, thought to be the "begetters of Evil" since Eve, were at once ruthless pursuers of men's power and virtually mentally deficient. These views were transmitted to the thirteenth century by monastic writers such as St. Bernard of Clairvaux and in the laws of medieval states. The famed thirteenth century legal scholar, Henry de Bracton (died 1268), himself an itinerant justice in the thirteenth century, was a legal repository of the negative views of women. Bracton demonstrated in his famous legal text, The Laws and Customs of England, that women were considered "inferior to men" because they had no real legal status. It is plausible to suggest, then, that English judges of the thirteenth and fourteenth centuries shared in this Bractonian world-view.

Gretchen had come to me two or three times within the past three months asking my advice on a particular school problem. The problem centered around a high school work/study student who intimidated many female teachers at my wife's school. Gretchen had told me pleadingly about the terribly uneasy feeling of being around Philip, the work/study student. Many of the teachers had read Philip's record of misbehavior and the fact that Philip was on criminal probation. Gretchen was desperately afraid that Philip was going to molest her or some other female at school. The Sunday evening before Cheryl's murder I had said, "He'll have to rape or kill someone before they will get him out of that school." Damn prophesy.

Gretchen, Cathy Sanders and Coach Jim Wall were lifeless when I arrived at the police station. Coach Wall had already given his testimony. When Gretchen's turn came, I was allowed to go into the interrogation room with her. The scene which she described was sickening. I immediately thought of Joan Seler in the fourteenth century. Yet, the graphics of Cheryl's rape and murder were even more alarming than those of the fourteenth century rape I had been reading. Innocent Cheryl, who had recently completed her undergraduate degree in elementary education at the midwestern university I was attending, was substituting in the library when she was attacked by Philip. He wasted little time executing his premeditated act. He ripped off her skirt, raped her, and then cut her to pieces with the razor blades he had purchased for the task. All of these facts were brought out by the prosecution in the relatively short trial in June, 1980.

In twentieth century America, rape becomes a public affair when it is reported to the authorities, when it becomes a statistic in a piece of research, or when it is reported to the populace through the various media (or when the victim is your friend or loved one). In the less sophisticated world of fourteenth century England, though the crime of rape could not have been as well-publicized, it had a tremendous impact on local society.

The stories of Joan and Cheryl did not end with the commission and prosecution of the crimes. The impact of rape was brutal, insensitive, continuous. Joan was a sexually-molested eleven year old. It is no idle speculation to suggest that her future life, and her parents' lives, were affected by the tragedy of rape. Joan had lost her virginity, an almost sure stigma for her in the marital marketplace. Barbara Hanawalt, in her book Crime and Conflict in English Communities, 1300-1348 (Harvard University Press, 1979) pointed to the almost total social ostracism that a raped female received from the villagers. Since marriage was extremely important for the female in thirteenth and fourteenth century English society, Joan's chances for a happy, successful married life were killed (even though Reymund de Limoges did not kill her). Cheryl Winter was not quite so lucky.

Philip Poteat was convicted of murder, but not of rape. In the state where the crime was committed, both felonies have to be committed on the same victim before the state invokes the death penalty. Murder, in this case, negated or superseded rape (indeed, when I read the news, I wondered how many rapes in medieval and modern times had been negated by murder, fear, or embarrassment). Cheryl Winter, twenty-one, newly graduated, recently married, was gone. Her young husband was, at least temporarily (and maybe permanently), psychologically dead. So were Gretchen and Cathy Sanders and all of Cheryl's family and friends. The impact of rape and murder (the impact, I think, was no greater because Cheryl had been murdered; it would have been equally as devastating had she been raped and not murdered) were nearly incapacitating for Gretchen (and Gretchen was just an acquaintance of Cheryl, a professional acquaintance). Gretchen could not sleep for two months. She would sit in our living room with the lights on late at night. She believed that she had a better chance of escape if she were attacked by a rapist than if she were "pinned" in our bedroom (being in a more restricted area obviously brought back thoughts of Cheryl's entrapment in the empty library). Needless to say, my career as a graduate student was affected. Dealing with the impact of this crime started to consume all our time and energies. We finally decided to move from the university town.

I received permission from understanding professors to do my dissertation in absentia. I have calculated that this crime added at least two years to my graduate work (I realize that this "loss" is negligible when compared to the loss of Cheryl's husband or parents; however, I am trying to emphasize the wide-ranging impact of rape).

Looking back at the rape of Joan Seler in the fourteenth century and at the brutal rape and murder of Cheryl Winter on St. Patrick's Day, 1980, my doctoral dissertation became a very personal, subjective matter. Even though I tried my best to remain as objective as possible (as all historians are taught to be), these two crimes haunted my work as the latter crime obviously haunted Gretchen's dreams.

I finished the dissertation and defended it at the university last November. I received the doctorate in January of 1983. Learning about the crime of rape and its impact on medieval English society was, unfortunately, made more brutally explicit and tragically clear by the rape and murder of my wife's professional associate. The stories of Joan and Cheryl, devastating as they were, serve as reminders that rape is a tragedy in any age.

The summer of 1980 was a time of soul searching once again. Should I go on? Will I be allowed to go on? How will I support us? Where can I find a job?

I applied for every job. When none were offered, I called Mr. Capezio in Cumberland County. Having done well for Capezio and Hawk, I thought that they might take me back. They said they would. However, just as I was about to take them up on their offer, the local school system, the Leaksville schools where I had gone, came through. I was offered a position as English teacher for Holland Junior High School. I took it.

Trying to write a dissertation at least two hours from an inadequate library is a tedious task. Doing it while teaching six classes a day to students who have a multiplicity of learning and emotional problems is near suicide. However, I promised myself that I had to do it. The transformation, as I had begun to see it, could not occur unless I plugged away. I believe that it was at this point that I wanted to be a teacher. Oh sure, I had gone through the motions for nine years, since 1971, but it was in 1980 that I began to see my role in the world of teaching and learning. I was on the road to synchronicity.

None of the seventh grade students under my direction seemed a bit impressed by my great feats of dissertating. They (and sometimes I believe I was among their number) didn't even know what the word meant or what the subject was all about. Sometimes, my committee confessed the same misgivings about me. Indeed, it was the strenuous teaching load coupled with the demands of writing and revision that began to take their toll — or did they? At first I thought that I was wearing thin, but that was before I began to battle fatigue with a more vigorous jogging and basketball program. In addition, I also sponsored the school literary club. I decided the best way to remain sane and to enjoy something about school was to rub elbows with a better quality of student. The literary club allowed me that luxury. Mr. Hummingbird, the principal, seemed pleased that I offered to sponsor another extra-curricular activity. Lord knows, the students needed a few more non-athletic activities.

When the announcement was made and when the students realized that the first meeting was during class time, they flocked to the cafeteria (site of the meeting) like animals boarding Noah's ark. I bemused that I was the Pied Piper. My ecstasy was shattered, like a dreaming man awakened by a thunderclap, when only thirty of the original 100 showed up for the next, and first, afterschool meeting. Yet, out of this crack group of thirty came a solid literary club. We met every two weeks, read original literature, discussed classical literature, and began to publish the school's first literary magazine, Straight from the Horse's Mouth.

As though I had planned it, a disc jockey from a local radio station called me after the news of the first magazine hit the local print media. He wanted the literary club to do a weekly radio show on literature. So, "Straight from the Horse's Mouth," a weekly radio show starring the Holland Junior High School Literary Club, was born. When a Space Cadet is hot, he's hot.

The chapter that should be the longest of the book — this one — is one of the shortest. However, I am planning a subsequent book on the trials and tribulations of the doctoral student. Watch for it in a theater near you!

CHAPTER SIXTEEN
THE ORIGINS OF CAPTAIN PROOFREADER

"John, you're a Space Cadet if I ever saw one," my not so friendly colleague at Holland Junior High School observed after seeing me run out of another colleague's classroom dressed in a black robe and hood, heinous devil mask, complete with three-toed monster feet and three-fingered monster hands.

"You'll have to speak up," I feigned deafness, "I can't hear very well under this get-up!"

"Oh, nothing," Mrs. Glamorpus said (I think she said that I was disgusting, although I knew she really loved my brain and body and wished that she had married me rather than the wimpy guy she's now stuck with).

I got two kicks out of Mrs. Glamorpus, who was a transplant from one of the northeastern states, a Yankee savior come South to bring culture to what she saw was a land decidedly lacking in couth. First of all, Mrs. Glamorpus, who had nearly succeeded in making her Southern-bawn (Southern for born) and bred colleagues believe she was a literary and educational messiah, held a deep-seated dislike for Southern dialect. Her hate, which oftentimes transcended the bounds of her attempt to suppress it, showed itself when I goaded her.

"Why did you come South to go to college?" I quizzed.

"Oh, it was cheaper," she grunted.

"Wouldn't a degree from Brown or Harvard or Penn mean more?" I dug deeper.

"Well, yes . . . but . . . there are so many applicants each year," she struggled.

"You mean you couldn't get into one of those schools and had to settle for a second-rate education in the South?" I asked with brutal frankness that surprised her.

"You Southerners are all alike!" she bellowed.

"You mean we all have Ph.D.'s, write books and articles, and are in the forefront of educational methodology like me?" I spun this back off the top of my head (some days are better than others).

"You're disgusting!" (didn't she already say that?), she shot back, turned abruptly, and left. I know she said that I was disgusting that time. I realize that I was a bit nasty but someone's got to do the dirty work of showing the world that Southerners are not all Boss Hoggs, Simon Legrees, and Jimmy Carters. There's more than one George Webber and Robert E. Lee.

Another time Mrs. Glamorpus articulated rather absurdly that Southern dialect and syntactical mistakes were synonymous. I began to see why Harvard and Brown had said "no."

"Tell me again, Mrs. G." I asked with delightful surprise, "say that again."

"Oh, you," she said, "everybody in town (and, of course, she meant, every Southerner) butchers the Queen's English by putting forth subject-verb disagreements: "I done this . . .", "He come over yesterday, etc., etc.," she explained with numerous examples.

"Do you mean that Southern people don't speak good?" I asked facetiously and grinned like a possum eating briars and she could tell that I was taunting her again.

"You think you're so smart, John," she said.

"I know I am!" I retorted.

An enraged look flushed her face.

"Missy (I called her Missy because her name was Melinda but, more importantly, because she hated the Southern penchant for giving everyone a nickname), why don't you get down off of your high horse, or, as my Mama would say, get your ass off of your shoulders and get on with the work you're trained to do — which is to educate those poah chilluns (Southern for 'poor children')," I turned from clown to counselor in a second or two.

"You're . . .", she began again.

"I know, I'm disgusting," I completed her sentence.

At least she would talk before I found out her (our) horrible (wonderful) secret: She had received a B.A. degree from the local university, but only after retaking freshman history a couple of times. The man who blew her ship out of the water was none other than Professor R. Hornblower Caribou, the man that I had worked under for an M.A. degree. When she realized that I had received all As, we talked very little. The cacophonous noise of what appeared to me a great paradox in our lives was deafening. Here was Miss Priss (a.k.a. Mrs. Glamorpus) trying to bring culture and enlightenment to a backwater of the desolate (in her eyes, anyway) South. The daughter of an upper echelon northeastern family, her father had a fine education, had traveled widely (with his family) in Europe, and had given his daughter everything. After barely getting through undergraduate school at a third-rate (her view) university (and after taking freshman history thrice — I found out that she had flunked it twice), she was loudly proclaiming herself to be the Messiah from the North (a kind of spiritual Gustavus Adolphus). On the other hand, I was a Ph.D. flake ("Space Cadet") from North Carolina, the son of a truck driver who had completed six years of schooling. My graduate education was financed by flipping pancakes at the International House of Pancakes and by teaching undergraduates at a first-rate Northern university where I was awarded prizes for my outstanding work in history. Could I keep my big mouth shut when this woman opened hers so frequently? Mrs. Glamorpus gave me a kick in that respect.

The other way that I got a kick out of Mrs. G. was her reference to me as a Space Cadet. It wasn't the first time. I remember when I was a guitar-playing Beatlemaniac who happened to play quarterback in high school, many people talked about me as a Space Cadet, a man who listened to a different snare drummer, who chose the road not taken, a . . . a . . . Space Cadet! Maybe Space Cadets are born . . .

The ground work was there. All those Space Cadets that had taught me since elementary school must have awakened that dormant quality in me. Mrs. Glamorpus simply triggered the Space Cadet forces within me, like a trickle of blood on the lips of Dracula.

Having only recently blown back into the city of LSD (Leaksville, Spray, and Draper, North Carolina were consolidated into Eden in

1967) in 1980, I was able to test the Thomas Wolfe Thesis: 'You can't go home again.' Wolfe aside, we needed a job. I finally begged a job out of the local superintendent. He placed me at Holland Junior High School as a language arts teacher. As my ordeal by fire, I was in charge of six classes of students (thirty to thirty-five in each class) who had a multiplicity of learning, social, and behavioral problems. I discovered that this was the initiation for new teachers in this school system. Frankly, I needed the job so badly and I had developed such confidence in my teaching abilities that I didn't care who I taught.

Yet, trying to write a dissertation from 6 p.m. to 11 p.m. after teaching six classes begins to have deleterious effects on an individual. Nevertheless, I really believed (and still do) that I owed the students and the school 110%. Those students were going to learn the English language.

I was thrown back onto my own resourcefulness, really more than I think is normal (whatever "normalcy" is in educational circles). I made games, developed behavioral modification schemes, threw them out, started again, and again, and again. Most of my days were filled with endless disciplinary actions for belligerent students, or students who could not adjust to my teaching.

After long soul searching near the end of January, after a semester of what I felt was getting nowhere, I reached a crisis. What was I going to do the rest of the semester? On top of it all, the chapters of the dissertation, the bureaucratic and clerical duties of the teacher, the domestic duties of the family, I had to undergo a teacher evaluation program for "new" teachers in the system. The fact that I had seven years of experience seemed to matter little to the administration. Since I had not taught in the LSD system before, I had never taught (that was their way of thinking). So, on top of everything else, I had to spend countless hours beings observed, videotaped, lectured to, and browbeaten. I decided that I would love it all.

"I always wanted to be on television," I laughingly responded to the assistant superintendent in charge of the evaluation program who tried to let me down easy with what he thought would be a disturbing invasion of academic freedom.

"Then you don't mind?" he asked as though he hoped I would mind.

"Not at all," I shot back.

"But, be ready for a whale of a show!" I promised.

Having made such a promise, reality hit me with the awful feeling that I was not prepared to offer a Busby Berkeley number. Thus, my crisis of late January, 1980. I decided to go to K-Mart. That's where I'd find a lesson plan that would impress students and teachers and administrators alike. Yet, what to do?

K-Mart, that temple of capitalist consumption. The television advertisement told me that I could find everything at K-Mart. So, I decided to go and look for a lesson plan.

As I stalked the aisles of the sterile, uniformly organized department store, I thought about what Mrs. Glamorpus had said the day that I wore the monster suit (see, I told you that I got two kicks out of her): "Space Cadet!"

"Space Cadet!" I may even have said the words aloud.

I think her appellation for me was brought to my consciousness as I walked through the toy section and my vision fell on the Star Wars characters that lined a shelf. I thought about Luke Skywalker, Han Solo, Chewbacca, and Obie Won and then, ZAP! A ray from some interplanetary mind control system hit me and I almost yelled out in true Herve Villechez fashion, "The Space Cadet!" "The Space Cadet!" Maybe I ought to be a Space Cadet, I began to get control of myself. Of course I should, I thought, I already am one! I always was one! But, what does a Space Cadet do?

Who was that masked man? At least I hope that was a mask he was wearing! I'm sorry, but it was not a mask. I ought to know, I'm Captain Proofreader!

Captain Proofreader appeared that lonely, crisis-ridden, evening in K-Mart. As I stalked the corridors of the famed department store hoping anxiously that a burst of creative energy would ease my lesson plan pain, I was drawn suddenly, almost magically, to a display of plastic space helmets. As if a force pulled my arms, I reached, grasped the black and silver helmet, and placed it gently upon my head.

I knew that I felt hot from the suspicious stares from the other customers. I tried to throw them off by suggesting that the helmet was for my little boy. None of them seemed convinced. Somehow, I had to do it.

I gathered up the helmet and floated into the sporting goods section not really knowing why I was in that particular section. Then, there it was! It was where it had always been, the same color, the same place. What it was was a bright orange rain suit for sportsmen. I had often wondered about the bright color. I decided that it must be used by pacifist deer hunters.

All I needed was a ray gun. I found one of those in the toy section and carried my gear to the checkout counter. I managed not to let my eyes meet the eyes of the lady at the cash register. She discreetly put the items in the transparent yellow K-Mart bag, handed it to me with the change, and I whisked out the door.

When I got home, I knew that I had the raw materials of a teaching breakthrough, but was puzzled about how to use it. What would the students think?

Trying to teach my 180 students the fine art of writing was one of my priorities. I decided to turn Captain Proofreader into the symbol of writing. Furthermore, I decided that if I were going to make headway with all 180 students, I needed their help, as peer evaluators.

I began the very next day. When the bell rang, the students made their way into my classroom. Atypically, I was not at the door to greet them. They knew something was amiss. Was I absent? Was there a substitute today? Had I taken a student to the office?

The tardy bell rang. Although the students were in their desks, they did not remember to refrain from talking. Some even stood up in the aisles. Then, the door opened. The talking stopped. There was a period of some countless seconds when nothing could be heard.

Then there was a giggle, looks of stunned disbelief, and finally some genuine horselaughs.

Captain Proofreader had made his debut. One thing was already accomplished. Captain Proofreader had gotten the attention of some of the most difficult students in school. Captain Proofreader said, "Hello, students." They even responded, as though they did not recognize the familiar face under the black and silver helmet. "Today we're going to zap the writing problem with Captain Proofreader's Extra-terrestrial English Laser (the two-dollar plastic raygun)," the Captain explained. The magic had already begun. The color and the outlandish idea were beginning to work their charm.

"And, students, you're going to help Captain Proofreader improve your own writing," he added. With those simple lines, and with some mouths still gaping, Captain Proofreader began to disseminate a peer evaluation practice sheet that he had created himself based on the Star Wars context. He decided that if students were going to be peer evaluators of their peers' writing, then they needed to practice evaluating writing. The peer evaluation practice sheet was called CAPTAIN PROOFREADER'S PEER WRITING ASSIGNMENT NUMBER ONE: "The Revenge of the Redeye" (a parody of "The Return of the Jedi"). Each student, according to Captain Proofreader's instructions, was to read the story and try to find the 35 grammatical and syntactical errors. Each student was to also make at least two positive comments about the piece. The story went like this:

Not too long ago

In a school

Not far from Spray (giggles immediately, the students realized that the story had a local setting, that got their interest immediately)

Captain Proofreader was called in to investigate strange abuses of language by Mr. J.C. Honeycut (the principal's last name was misspelled; was the principal the abuser of the language?), principle of Holmes junior high school; (principal misspelled, the first letter in junior, high, and school should be capitalized; the sentence should end with a period). It seems that many members of the school were

122

using English that would embarrass your average hoodlums: Principle Honicutt vowed to clear up this calamity. (period after hoodlums, principal and Honeycutt misspelled) Which was a terrible imidge for the school? (sentence fragment, image misspelled, period instead of question mark). Captain Proofreader had not been seen at Holland Junior High since mid-October, 1980. He had been quartered at his famus Fountain of Couth, a veritable refreshing haven for cultured and linguistically-skilled aesthetes. (here the students should have discovered that a new paragraph had begun with Captain Proofreader had not been indented . . . ; famous is misspelled; aesthetes sent many to the dictionary). _____ (add your own character; this was a particular favorite of the students. They could add anyone they wanted to in the blank spaces) was sent by Mr. Honicutt to summon Captain Proofreader. When _____ got to the Fountain of Couth, he explained to Proofreader; "Cap, we need your help desparately!" (comma should be after Proofreader; desperately is misspelled).

?Holland Junior High is sinking into a mire of non-standard English? he added (quotation marks instead of question marks). 'That mean old English corrupter, _____ (add your own character), is ruining everyone,' he went on. (double quotation marks instead of single are needed).

"My goodness!" exclaimed Proofreader. "Let me get my Extra-terrestrial English Laser," he added. With a rapid movement. He grabbed the deadly-looking weapon and galumphed out of the cavern door. ("With a rapid . . . " is a fragment. There should be a comma after movement; the h in He should be lower case; galumphed created problems for those who had forgotten their "Jabberwocky"; and, of course, the paragraph should be indented).

Captain Proofreader and _____ parked the Couthmobile in front of the school near _____'s (again, add your own names in the blanks) pink Cadillac and walked inside. _____ met them at the door and thanked Captain Proofreader for giving up his gig at the C.B. Hut to come. (the C.B. Hut is a local dive that the local students know) "My how things have changed since i was here last?" exclaimed Proofreader. (the "I" should be capitalized; an exclamation mark instead of a question mark). "Are the Guitar and Tambourine students still over in room 411!" inquired the Captain. (Guitar and Tambourine students refers to the G.T. — gifted and talented — students; question mark rather than an exclamation mark). "Why, yes they are!" said _____ (the student fills in here with his own Holland Junior High character). "Maybe we can hear them play later, C.P.," _____ added.

So, Cap, Mr. H., and _____ (another fill-in) met for an hour about the terrible degeneration of language at school. Finally, Mr. H. came up with an idea? (period instead of a question mark at the end of the sentence). "Cap, why don't you go and seek guidance from the Redeye Master at Reid's House?" suggested the Principle: (Principal is misspelled; the Redeye Master is the proprietor of a "greasy spoon restaurant in Eden called Reid's House). Captain Proofreader fed the mice under the hood of the Couthmobile and sped off. (the student should state that this paragraph should have been indented).

Captain Proofreader got out of the Couthmobile and strolled into Reid's House. Everyone there were wearing either a sky-blue University of North Carolina cap or a Farm-All cap. (incorrect subject-verb agreement — Mrs. Glamorpus was partially correct in her estimation of the locals). He could not understand how a place like this was the home of a Redeye Master. (Redeye Master is, of course, a parody of the Jedi Master in the "Star Wars" movies. Again, students should have noticed that the paragraph was not indented).

After a few minutes, Reid and his friend _____ (another fill-in) appeared from the smoke and grease. They did not speak but Proofreader knew that he was in the presence of some strange power. Through telepathy, Reid instructed Proofreader. Proofreader gazed around the room and: with the sheer strength of his new-found power: levitated all of the caps off the heads of their wearers. (the two colons should be deleted). But, his strength ebbed and the caps fell down into the bowls of beans, the Master Burger plates, and the coconut creem pies. (cream is misspelled). Telepathically Reid told Proofreader that he needed the help of a further special power.

Immediately a waitress brought C.P. a plate laden with scrambled eggs, grits, and what appeared to be the reddest ham C.P. had ever seen, smothered in redeye gravy? (the sentence should end with a period). Proofreader blurted out, ? Reid, this ham is as red as deer meat:" (the spoken words should be placed within quotation marks instead of between a question mark and a colon; an exclamation mark should replace the colon). "You're close," responded Reid. The more Proofreader ate, the more nauseous he became. Finally, he could take no more, language or not. He struggled to the Couthmobile. Reid yelled to him, "May the horse be with you!" Now Proofreader knew the secret of the Redeye!

TO BE CONTINUED . . .

The method worked. The students liked and appreciated my willingness to entertain, to let my hair down, to be different, to take a chance. They learned and learned and learned. I asked myself, "Why haven't I done this before — or something like it?" Captain Proofreader, in some almost magical way, made for a more wholesome classroom environment.

I devised numerous activities based on Captain Proofreader. However, I realized that I shouldn't run a good thing in the ground, so I only came to school dressed as C.P. three times that semester. But, the anticipation of the students' wondering when Captain Proofreader would be back, being intrigued by the work they were doing, and genuinely proud of their unorthodox teacher for having the guts (or lack of brains) to follow his own corny impulses made C.P. a living part of everyday. When my slowest class, all of whom were in the seventh grade but reading on a first or second grade level, wrote their own outer space story on the parts of speech, acted it out, and filmed it, I knew that Cap Proofreader had arrived as a teacher. Captain Proofreader was a hit. I knew it when the principal called me in to his office near the end of the semester to ask if I would be interested in moving to the eighth grade for the next year (I asked him if he meant to be a teacher or a student?) to teach the gifted and talented (now, a.k.a. Academically Gifted, although I always referred to them as my Guitar and Tambourine classes because I believed in mainstreaming and I was not wanting to be a party to establishing a snob-ridden, artificial educational aristocracy). Maybe, I thought, there is a place for a Space Cadet after all?

I found out through the all-too effective grapevine known as the teacher's lounge that Mrs. Glamorpus was furious at my new duties because she wanted the G.T. job. The rumor became a proven fact when Mrs. G. never spoke to me again unless she saw me in the girls' bathroom (where I was after illegal smokers) or, at Halloween, when I would wear my black robe and hood, devil mask, and hands and feet, into her quiet, traditional classroom and scare the daylights out of some unsuspecting student who loved it. Mrs. G. would say in rather disgusted fashion, "That's Mr. Carter (she refused to acknowledge my Ph.D. and she loved to give away my identity to spoil my fun and the kids' Halloween fun), class, he's such a Space Cadet!" The students would get quiet, sensing that something was a bit amiss. They all turned to me for a retort to Mrs. G's statement. I would roll my eyes behind the mask. Their grins told me they understood and then I would whisk out of the class in my best Christopher Lee move.

CHAPTER SEVENTEEN
LEADING THE MAGICAL TRANSFORMATION TOUR

Nineteen-eighty-two was a very good year. Gretchen and I bought a big, rambling colonial house and began to renovate it — er, transform it. I finally persuaded my doctoral committee that my dissertation on crime in medieval society was passable. And, I passed through a very important stage of my transformation as a teacher.

As you have seen in the last two chapters, I have been talking about transforming as though I recognized it coming. Even though I had intuitive feelings that things were happening, I did not realize until the stages had been transcended that I was being transformed.

Yet, by 1982, I knew that my success in teaching was a synthesis of knowledge imparted from past Space Cadets coupled with the recognition of my own ability to contribute — the self-realization that I had the "write" stuff. Oh, it was a Luke Skywalker-type awakening all right!

The summer of '82 was a very special time in my transformation. I was invited to attend the new Writing Project at a local university, to be a part of twenty-five teachers of writing in a team which would improve the abilities of teachers to teach writing. The Bay Area writing project that began in San Francisco in 1973 had finally made its way — a decade later — to the opposite coast of America. The experience of the writing project came at the best time because of my knowing that transformation was at work. I was ready to absorb the wisdom as it beamed in on me.

My summer with twenty-five colleagues, many of them Space Cadets themselves, was an emotional, almost mystical union made up of many transforming teachers like myself. We learned a considerable amount from each other.

After our summer of incubation, we emerged from our old shells ready to spread the gospel of the writing process. I spent almost as much time on the road in the 1982-83 school year as I did in my own Gifted and Talented English classes at Holland Junior High. I traveled the width and length of the state. I talked incessantly to teachers about the nuances and self-actualization of the writing process.

My teachings led me to write four books on the subject during this flurry of about one calendar year. They were: Captain Proofreader's Foolproof Writing Program; E.T. (English Teacher) in the Content Areas: A Plan for Writing Across the Curriculum; Captain Proofreader's Sixty Ways to Zap Reluctant Writers; and, Captain Proofreader's Guide to the Writing Process.

Wherever I went, I carried my alter-ego, Captain Proofreader, along. C.P. became synonymous with the writing process in my state. About halfway through my talks to teachers, I would tell them that the next series of activities required an assistant. I excused myself and went into the hallway outside of the classroom, and donned the stunning orange space suit, helmet, and Extra-terrestrial English Laser. I dashed back into the lecture room, sprayed some imaginary rays with the English Laser, and told them my tales of transformation. They beamed, just like the students had done when I jumped out of the closet in the classroom. After each session, the participants gobbled up my books and thanked me for my performance. I received a letter from four teachers in another part of the state who reported tremendous successes with their students. The enclosed pictures of the four teachers, who ranged in age from thirty to sixty-two, showed them dressed in monster outfits or space suits each bearing a name like Princess Pronunciation, Grammar Gorilla, or Lieutenant Language. I smiled a long, contented smile of tranformation.

Educational and social tranformation are aptly characterized in Marilyn Ferguson's famous book, The Aquarian Conspiracy. As she explains, when a transforming person or organization is in process, it naturally runs into conflict with older ways of doing. As new ways of thinking and acting begin to be accepted, they run counter to the older laws. I think this happened to me at Holland Junior High School.

I was "getting more ink" in the local and regional papers than anyone or anything else. When the regional paper ran a cover story of Captain Proofreader, the beginning of the end (of one phase) was at hand. Pretty soon, my superiors (their term) in the administrative office were making it difficult for me to leave my classes to give workshops or make talks around the state. They came up with absurd reasons. I believe they were jealous. But I also believe that my transforming ideas and methods ran contrary to their thought patterns. It soon became obvious that I would have to go. But, there was one transformation goal to accomplish. I wanted to create a teacher rock band to demonstrate that teachers are not one-dimensional fuddy-duddies. I went to work. I did not know how much time I had. My dissertation done, I began to search out college and university teaching jobs.

CHAPTER EIGHTEEN
BLAH NA NA AND BEYOND

My transformation included the creation of many activities that would have surprised me had I heard about them ten years earlier. Now, I was doing things which I never learned in undergraduate school, per se. But, by constantly reading, daring, and by occasionally being in contact with other Space Cadets (from elementary school to the Ph.D.), I began to burst forth from that past that stifles us all. Captain Proofreader not only symbolized the writing process for me, but a whole way of educating — maybe a holistic way of education (some of my colleagues suggested that I had created an assholistic type of education).

I had gone through many stages of transformation and the emergence of Captain Proofreader helped me recognize my own transformation. I ran afoul of any administration mired in mediocrity and strapped by philosophies of learning and teaching that were, at best, unsuited for the 1980s.

Before I left Holland Junior High School for the outer limits of learning, I brought together individuals, from across the curriculum to establish a very positive model of teachers. I had wanted to create a teacher rock band in the 1970s while I was a teacher at Winner Junior High School in Cumberland County but the Ph.D. Siren sang and I just had to obey.

Teachers are often pigeon-holed as rather uncreative types who "teach because they can't do." Remember when you were spotted in the supermarket by one of your students who gawked at you because he thought teachers only graded papers. He didn't realize that they actually ate as well! The first year that I taught, I learned that not only do students stereotype teachers, teachers stereotype teachers. As a history teacher and a former history student who had had to write more than his shsare, I believed that I could teach my kids a thing or two about writing, footnoting, and paraphrasing. After word leaked out to the English teachers at my school that a history teacher was cutting in on their turf, some of the English colleagues went to visit the principal.

My point is that teachers should not be stereotyped. They live, breathe, have dreams, and pay bills just like everyone else. But, sometimes they really don't act like everyone else. One reason, of course, is the stereotypical view of teachers: the English teacher with wire-rimmed glasses and a little bun of hair at the crown of her head; the physical education teacher who only knows how to teach the "fast break"; the science teacher who needs a lesson in the humanities; the social studies teacher who also teaches the "fast break" because he is also the boys' basketball coach; the principal who shuffles papers; the guidance counselor who specializes in disappearing. Needless to say, many of these stereotypes are based in fact. yet, there are always those teachers who are multi-dimensional characters who can do lots of things. They teach because they want to teach, they care enough about kids and civilization to offer themselves.

I am going to tell you about a group of junior high school teachers (at Holmes Junior High School in Eden, North Carolina) who are multi-dimensional. Their creativity shone forth most brightly in the creation of a rock band and blitzed the blahs at the school for three years.

Blah Na Na got its name, obviously, from the well-known group Sha Na Na, whose nostalgia for the 1950s has been part of a nation-wide 50s craze for almost a decade. Once the subject was dropped, it was not long before the latent talent and ham-ism of the group surfaced and became a dynamic force which united the disparate participants into an honest-to-goodness rock band.

The first "gig" was set for February 13, 1981, a Friday before Valentine's Day that was set aside for the annual Talent Show. The students in the show had practiced long and hard. But, in addition to the regular talent show, there was an exciting air of electricity about a "visiting" rock group called Blah Na Na who would entertain while the judges made their decisions about the student talent winners.

Unknown to the students, the band members were none other than teachers at Holmes Junior High School: John Marshall Carter, English teacher; Peter Cunningham, social studies teacher; Wayne

Tuggle, science teacher; Bill Burton, science teacher; Arlyn Bunch, physical education teacher; Braxton Rumbley, physical education teacher; Duane Best, choral director; Wayne Barnett, band director; Larry Kendrick, social studies teacher; guidance counselor Sara Stultz; Wayne Seymour, English teacher. The teachers practiced hard for a month, spending as much time as four hours a night, three nights a week. Carter, Tuggle, Best, Barnett, Kendrick, and Seymour were musicians in their own right. None had ever played together before. But, they knew if school were to be more than just a place to come and be brow-beaten for eight hours a day, they had to do it — and do it right. Soon, the practice session became consuming passions.

A week before the show was to go on, the group talked local businesses into helping. Some local restaurants agreed to put welcome signs on their marquees (WELCOME BLAH NA NA FEBRUARY 13, 1981). The local papers ran articles about the mystery band that was to play at Morehead Auditorium (the high school auditorium across the street from Holmes Junior High). Furthermore, Fair's Funeral Home agreed to lend the "band" one of their silver limousines.

Finally, the last rehearsal came. Everything was set to go. The "band" was to actually play all the music and sing well known songs from the 1950s and early 1960s. Carter was on guitar; Tuggle on guitar; Kendrick on piano; Best on synthesizer; Seymour on bass; Barnett on drums; the remaining teachers put together a dance routine that would have impressed Smokey Robinson and the Miracles. The whole group dressed accordingly. Sha Na Na would have been proud of their clones, Blah, Na Na. Even a bulletin board in the main hall asked "Who is Blah Na Na?" All the students were abuzz. Carter became "Dr. J" Carter (he has just attained his Ph.D.); Tuggle was dubbed "Be-Bop-A-Lu-La"; Rumbley was "Bruiser"; Burton was "Bare Knuckles"; Best was "Yellow Bird"; Stultz was "Big Bad Mama"; Seymour was "Sizzling"; Barnett was "Skins"; Kendrick was "Jerry Lee"; Cunningham was "Wild Man." All fifties rockers had to have nicknames, didn't they?

The repertoire was perfect. "Johnnie B. Goode," the famous Chuck Berry number; "Teen Angel", a tune by Tuggle that brought down the house; "Blue Suede Shoes"; "Whole Lotta Shakin' Going On"; "Twist and Shout"; "The Twist"; "Why Must I Be a Teenager in Love"; "Goodnight Sweetheart", the tune used by Sha Na Na as their theme song, and "Only Sixteen."

When the assistant principal introduced the "band", there was still an aura of mystery hanging over the auditorium. All the audience knew to do was to respond spontaneously — and loud! The band was a visual and musical success. The band played to a thunderous uproar from the crowd of two thousand students, parents, and school administrators. For about an hour, teachers and students were communicating in a way very rarely achieved at any educational level. Then, it ended. The show was over. But all was not forgotten.

For three years now, Blah Na Na has made annual appearances. Each year the thrill is there. Mr. Tuggle, Mr. Rumbley, and the rest become super heroes for a day. They and their colleagues win the respect of their students. They have run no risk of losing control of their classes because they have "let their hair down" (or, should I say, greased their hair back). They have proven that they are more than science, English, and social studies teachers and guidance counselors, and band and choral directors. They have shown their students, colleagues, and community that they are multi-dimensional, caring, cooperative professionals who have tried, like so many good teachers, to make learning and living wholesome, and fun.

Look around your school. There are closet musicians waiting to mesmerize. There are closet novelists who want to talk about writing. There is a rather large supply of talent — maybe not "certified," but talent, nevertheless — waiting for the right combination of forces to weld it into a unified and enthralling dynamic. Look around. Talk it up. It's good for the Blahs.

All things must pass (according to George Harrison and a hundred or so others). The good things that I helped to create for students at Holland Junior High School and the transformational awakening which finally came to me in the early 1980s were important stages of growth for me. Yet, it was time to travel on. I had probably done all I could do in that environment.

In May of 1983, I accepted a professorship at Georgia Southern College in Statesboro, Georgia. I left Holland and headed for the next stage of transformation. I see, I think, what I am becoming up ahead in the future and I am now preparing to give chase. In looking back at my transformation, I must give thanks to the men and women who helped me, either directly or indirectly, to realize that I was what I always wanted to be, that I had to discover that reality for myself. It is to this group of Space Cadets that I owe thanks.

ABOUT THE AUTHOR

John Marshall Carter was born in Leaksville, North Carolina on April 6, 1949. He is the third of three children of Howard C. and Virginia Carter. He received his A.B. from Elon College, an M.A. in history from the University of North Carolina at Greensboro, and a Ph.D. in history from the University of Illinois at Urbana-Champaign. Dr. Carter has taught, supervised, and coached at the middle, junior high, and high school levels. He was a teacher in the public schools of Virginia, North Carolina, and Illinois before becoming a university professor. Although he is a medievalist in the Department of History at East Carolina University, he is called upon to supervise student teachers. In addition to his work as a medievalist, he contributes pedagogical articles to educational journals such as SOCIAL EDUCATION, ENGLISH JOURNAL, THE CLEARINGHOUSE, and others. He has published numerous articles in history and education. Dr. Carter is is the author of RAPE IN MEDIEVAL ENGLAND: AN HISTORICAL AND SOCIOLOGICAL STUDY (University Press of America), THE BAYEUX TAPESTRY AS A SOCIAL DOCUMENT (Ginn Press), and SPORTS AND PASTIMES OF THE MIDDLE AGES (Brentwood Publishers). He is presently working on an extensive monograph entitled SPORTS IN THE MIDDLE AGES for Greenwood Press.

Dr. Carter has received grants from the National Endowment for the Humanities and from the Deutscher Akademischer Austauschdienst. His hobbies include basketball, fishing, songwriting, and performing in a folk-rock band called THE WAMPUS CATS. The band has released a single and is now working on an album.

Dr. Carter's wife is Suzon Grogan Carter and they have a daughter, Alyson.